# INFECTED

### How to Stop the Global Spread of Rage, Deception and Insanity

*Karen Hardin*

**PALADIN**
PUBLISHING

Karen has great insight into the spiritual climate of our nation and shares it in an engaging and convincing way. Her ability to see the bigger picture with a spiritual lens is a gift. Karen's massive library of writings have blessed millions around the globe for years. This book will greatly add to this library; it is chock full of that valuable wisdom.

**Dave Kubal**
**President/CEO**
**Intercessors for America**

---

Karen Hardin is not afraid to confront controversial issues or challenge the mainstream narrative. In her book, *Infected,* Karen uncovers the deceptive tactics of the enemy playing out on the national scene to reveal the deeper spiritual conditions of the heart.

In reading this book, you will not only be given effective spiritual tools for warfare, you will be given practical application of these principles to stop the spread of toxic lies and deadly deception that are eating our nation alive. The eye-opening treatment Karen provides may be shocking to some, but will bring life and health to those with ears to hear and hearts ready to respond.

**Wanda Alger**
**Fivefold prophet, pastor's wife, speaker**
**Author of five books including**
***Moving from Sword to Scepter***

Karen Hardin has written a marvelous book, or more correctly, a road map to help us navigate through these infectious times. I have often mused over why this culture had such an obsession with zombies until recent days. Karen describes with pinpoint clarity the real infection running rampant in our world, an infection that results in zombie-like symptoms—anger, rage, insanity, and a murderous spirit. Now more than ever we must heed Proverbs 4:23: "Keep your heart with all diligence, for out of it spring the issues of life.[1]" Karen shows us how.

**Craig Walker — Lead pastor**
**Upward Church and author of**
***Catch* and *Born for the Extraordinary***

---

I have known Karen for many years and appreciate her heart for God, her commitment to solid doctrinal teaching, her compassion towards people and her courage and character to speak and demonstrate truth when it may not be convenient or politically correct.

The truths brought forward and issues confronted in this book are a wake-up call to the days and times in which we live and the need for boldness and clarity to see and respond with spiritual insight and boldness in order for our voices and actions to break the darkness that is trying to overwhelm this present generation and bring a dullness to our senses and apathy in our attitudes.

We have watched churches grow in size, but shrink in their influence in our cities and states. No longer can we be content with our services and not realize we need to fight for our nation.

**Paul Chase — Founder, president and senior pastor**
**Keys to Freedom Ministries and Alabang New Life**
**Christian Center (Philippines)**

---

As a fellow writer, I have worked closely with Karen Hardin for several years. While I have read many things she has written, this book portrays a deeper level of writing excellence. It is insightful, revelatory, and anointed. I could not put it down. *Infected* is a must read for every Christian.

**Kim Potter — President**
**A New Thing Ministries**

---

*Infected* engages the reader from the start! Karen Hardin makes the complicated uncomplicated, tracing the link from the national chaos to the brokenness and depravity of every human heart. But be encouraged, she shares the remedy, the "vaccine" for us all.

**Judy McDonough**
**Director of Communications**
**Intercessors for America**

*INFECTED: How to Stop the Global Spread of Rage, Deception and Insanity*
ISBN 978-0-9911578-2-2
Copyright © 2021 by Karen Hardin
P. O. Box 700515
Tulsa, OK 74170

Published by Paladin Publishing
Represented by PriorityPR Group & Literary Agency.
www.prioritypr.org

Text Design: Lisa Simpson

One person really can change the world. The reason the world was sequestered into home sheltering this first half of 2020 was because of the infectious nature of one individual. That one who touches one who in turn touches another causes a chain reaction that can literally infect the world.

Jesus demonstrated the power of one every time He stopped for the one. Jesus understood that one person plus God is a majority in any situation. You are the salt of the earth. You are the light of the world. You are a city on a hill that cannot be hidden. You are the yeast of the kingdom of God. You are those who have turned the world upside down, and you do it every time that you stop for the one.

— Dan McCollam, Best-selling author
and Founder of Prophetic Company Global

# DEDICATION

To the One who will never self-distance from us. He will be with us no matter where we are, what we are doing and no matter how bad it looks.

He is in our midst and is performing a turnaround.

# CONTENTS

# INTRODUCTION

It shouldn't have surprised me. When I finally sat down to begin to write this book, I was inundated with issues that came out of the blue which were opportunities to take offense. In fact, I told a friend that in a ten-day period while writing, I had more opportunities for offense than the previous two years combined. It was the virus working to gain a foothold.

Offense is the second step of a deadly spiritual progression that can be seen over and over again in history. That same spiritual progression is taking place in our world today. And once we allow offense to take hold of us, it always leads us into deception. Always.

In fact, it is all around us. And the problem is those infected don't even realize it.

If you are reading this book, you are looking for insight. But I can tell you that there will be a significant number of readers who will take offense at this teaching and close it before finishing the book. I encourage you to push away the opportunity to be offended which opens the door to deception. Are you willing to look at this spiritual virus to see how it operates, and even more importantly, to find out if you are infected?

We all have been at one time or another. And the only way to walk free in this hour is to remove it from our lives. Let me show you how.

## Chapter 1

# INFECTED

Although the world has been rocked by the COVID-19 virus, it pales compared to the infection rate of a greater virus running rampant, infecting millions, and which has been completely ignored. If left untreated and allowed to run its course, it ends in insanity. And the infected are everywhere. It is seen clearly as we reflect back over instances of violence taking place in our nation over recent months.

"These people had evil in their eyes as they surrounded us. They would stop at nothing," Senator Rand Paul stated after he and his wife were surrounded by an angry mob on the streets of Washington, D.C.

Rand's wife, Kelley, described the terrifying situation even more vividly in a piece she wrote for the *Washington Examiner*:

"The mob swarmed me and my husband in a tight circle, screaming expletives, threats, and shouting, 'Say her name,' (referring to Breonna Taylor). We rushed up to two police officers, and I believe that is the only thing that kept us from being knocked to the ground. Even pressed against the officers, we were greatly outnumbered.

"As the mob grew and became more threatening, we literally could not move, and neither could the two officers for several minutes. The rioters were inches from us, screaming in our faces.

"That was the worst part. At first, I attempted to meet the eyes of one of the protesters and tried to explain that Rand authored the Justice for Breonna Taylor Act, but it seemed to just infuriate them more, as they called me a 'bitch' and 'racist wh---' alongside an endless torrent of 'f--- yous.'

"Mobs are terrifying. They looked at us with no humanity—just a vicious and righteous zeal. After that, I just kept my eyes down and prayed. All I could think of was the driver who was pulled from his car, viciously kicked in the head and left lying in his own blood in

Portland, Oregon, last week. . . ."[2]

The Rand's are certainly not the only ones who have felt their lives were threatened as they walked the streets of America.

This summer a twenty-four-year-old man was brutally attacked outside a convenience store in Texas by five men who followed him out of the store. The man was waiting in line to buy groceries when a group of men cut in front of him.

**"Mobs are terrifying.
They looked at us with no humanity—
just a vicious and righteous zeal.**

"I looked over and said, 'There's a line for a reason,'" he explained. Evidently that was enough to provoke their rage as they began to mock his hair and clothes.

As soon as he exited the store, he was attacked.[3]

In August, Black Lives Matter protesters confronted and harassed people eating outside at restaurants in Washington, D.C. as they shouted, "White silence is violence!" and screamed in their faces.

One video showed protesters demanding a woman raise her fist to show her solidarity for the BLM cause. "I felt I was under attack," the woman told *Washington Post* reporter Fredrick Kunkle. When she did not comply with their demand, they screamed in her face, without masks, to intimidate her into submission. The irony is the woman *did* support Black Lives Matter, but felt she should not be forced into an inauthentic action.[4]

How many times a day have you heard a comment, seen a news clip or engaged in a conversation and thought, "Are those people insane?" Rage, violence and insanity are all around us. The questions are, Where does it come from, and how did it start?

The world has turned topsy-turvy as we look for answers to the COVID-19 pandemic and how to stem the infection rate. It has taken our eyes off a more deadly spiritual virus whose infection rate is far greater. I look around and see its results everywhere. But unlike COVID-19, there doesn't seem to be any awareness of this disease or how to stem the tide. As a result, it has gone unchecked and wrecked-havoc. It is the true pandemic, and it is deadly.

This spiritual virus, like any disease, has a progression. If left untreated, it will run its course of destruction in the life of its host. The final stage is insanity; and it can be seen all around us, its victims raging and wild-eyed like the attackers in the previous stories.

We see it on the news, on social media, and at the office where conversations escalate exponentially into an enraged response. Think back to your own experience where you have unknowingly encountered this virus. Where there has been a disproportionally angry or emotional response to a situation, and the palatable rage feels like a slap across the face. Caught off guard, we wonder what to do stunned at what just happened probably much like the Paul family or the patrons in the restaurant who were confronted simply for being there. When we encounter such rage, no attempt to assuage it will suffice because the issue is not a person, but a spiritual root.

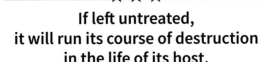

**If left untreated,
it will run its course of destruction
in the life of its host.**

Unfortunately, the problem in those interactions is you have also now been exposed! What you do next determines infection.

## INFECTION

(Have you been infected? Take the virus test at the back of the book to find out.)

Where does infection begin? There are multiple points of entry. It can begin with an attitude, offense, or jealousy over someone or something. It can occur when we experience unjust outbursts or attacks, which can plant a seed of offense in the soil of our hearts. Perhaps it is the certainty of being right on an issue which can then spread to pride, which opens the door to deception. It would surprise you how easily we can be infected without recognizing it.

**It would surprise you how easily we can be infected without recognizing it.**

## THE PROGRESSION

What is the progression of this virus? It can be seen over and over both past and present. It has continued from one generation to another because the needed "vaccine" is often overlooked or rejected.

We can easily see the symptoms—offense, rage, murderous intent to name a few. But they are simply indicators of the deeper problem infecting the heart.

This spiritual virus is far more deadly than COVID-19 or Ebola. Its death rate, unless the cycle is stopped, is 100 percent. The tragedy is many are infected and don't even realize it. Recognizing infection is critical in obtaining the cure. But that can be difficult.

This is how I discovered the existence of this spiritual virus.

Several years ago, I was in a business relationship with four individuals. At the time I would have called them close friends. Until one day, all four relationships started to head south at a dramatic rate—all at the exact same time—for reasons that didn't make sense. It was nothing short of bizarre. It was like someone flipped a switch and crazy took over. The outrage I encountered was highly disproportionate to any issue on the table. Phone calls turned into verbal lashings and accusations. Business contracts were broken. I called each one to have a conversation and uncover the root behind the sudden shift. Even that triggered anger and justification of their actions. All were Christians. One of the individuals was president of a ministry and responded, "I train people how to avoid anger and conflict. I'm *not* angry and I *don't* need to talk to you," she insisted when I called to suggest we go for coffee and discuss the contention between us. Rather than having a conversation to discuss the issue, she doubled down completely convinced she was acting in a "godly" manner.

The harder I worked to see these relationships repaired, the deeper the damage as anger turned to rage. But it didn't stop there. Eventually it turned to murderous intent to destroy my business, if not me. I sought counsel and advice from numerous sources to gain insight into the bizarre behaviors that had erupted. But all to no avail. No one had any concrete insights after I explained the situations I was encountering. I spent hours in prayer seeking answers and healing for my wounded heart and lost relationships. It was in that wilderness setting that the Holy Spirit revealed to me the ancient virus and its deadly progression. It has existed from the beginning of time and is rampant still today. Its effects can be seen across the globe.

**It was in that wilderness setting
that the Holy Spirit revealed to me
the ancient virus and its deadly progression.**

This is how it starts.

## Chapter 2

# THE ROOT

"Pride must die in you or nothing
of Heaven can live in you."
—Andrew Murray

*"For the Lord preserves the faithful, but abundantly
repays the one who acts in pride."*

Psalm 31:23 ESV

This spiritual virus is not new. It is just often overlooked. It has been around since ancient times—but never in my lifetime to such a pandemic state. The riots and mob actions which have filled our cities are symptoms and indicators of its presence. We can look back in history to see a vivid example of the virus's progression and the mob rage it creates.

Back in the days of the first century church, Paul, formerly Saul, encountered this virus time and again. One such instance is found in Acts 19.

*"About that time there arose a great disturbance about the Way. A silversmith named Demetrius, who made silver shrines of Artemis, brought in a lot of business for the craftsmen there. He called them together, along with the workers in related trades, and said: 'You know, my friends, that we receive a good income from this business. And you see and hear how this fellow Paul has convinced and led astray large numbers of people here in Ephesus and in practically the whole province of Asia. He says that gods made by human hands are no gods at all. There is danger not only that our trade will lose its good name, but also that the temple of the great goddess Artemis will be discredited; and the goddess herself, who is worshiped throughout the province of Asia and the world, will be robbed of her divine majesty.'*

*When they heard this, they were furious and began shouting, 'Great is Artemis of the Ephesians!' Soon the whole city was in an uproar. The people seized Gaius and Aristarchus, Paul's traveling companions from Macedonian, and all of them rushed into the theater together.. Paul wanted to appear before the* crowd, but the disciples would not let him. Even some of the officials of the province, friends of Paul, sent him a message begging him not to venture into the theater.

The assembly was in confusion: Some were shouting one thing, some another. Most of the people did not even know why they were there. The Jews in the crowd pushed Alexander to the front, and they shouted instructions to him. He motioned for silence in order to make a defense before the people. But when they realized he was a Jew, they all shouted in unison for about two hours: "Great is Artemis of the Ephesians!"

The city clerk quieted the crowd and said: "Fellow Ephesians, doesn't all the world know that the city of Ephesus is the guardian of the temple of the great Artemis and of her image, which fell from heaven? Therefore, since these facts are undeniable, you ought to calm down and not do anything rash. You have brought these men here, though they have neither robbed temples nor blasphemed our goddess. If, then, Demetrius and his fellow craftsmen have a grievance against anybody, the courts are open and there are proconsuls. They can press charges. If there is anything further you want to bring up, it must be settled in a legal assembly. As it is, we are *in danger of being charged with rioting because of what happened today. In that case we would not be able to account for this commotion, since there is no reason for it." After he had said this, he dismissed the assembly.*[5]

In this story, the symptoms and indicators can be clearly seen when you recognize the progression. First, we need to look closely at Demetrius's actions and words which reveal three symptoms and the root of infection.

1. Pride – (root)

2. Jealousy

3. Greed

By his words, Demetrius reveals the emotions which control him. But they are more than just emotions. They are spiritual strongholds that have taken root in his life and now guide his actions. Like a physical virus which lodges into our systems and incubates until it produces an outward manifestation of illness, it is the same with a spiritual virus. It first lodges into our heart and mind, incubates and then produces an outward manifestation.

Demetrius was a leader in both his craft and social standing in the city. He was a man of wealth and recognized that if Paul entered their city and turned people's hearts to God and away from the worship of Artemis, his livelihood and social standing would be negatively impacted. This is where we see the seeds of pride and jealousy within him. Pride in what he did and in his position, jealousy that Paul might interrupt his prosperous business and position in the community. Greed was certainly part of the mix that controlled Demetrius's heart as he told his peers, "You know, my friends, that we receive a good income from this business."[6]

**Like a physical virus which lodges into our systems and incubates until it produces an outward manifestation of illness, it is the same with a spiritual virus.**

(Note: This is the part of the root behind the ongoing battle to keep abortion legal. Like Demetrius, those involved recognize that their ongoing prosperity and funding depend on the business and will do anything in their power to keep it intact. Their actions are fueled by this virus. And the next stage of the virus reveals how they can continue to promote the murder of innocent babies as "choice.")

Pride and jealousy work closely together. Where one is found, the other is lurking nearby. Demetrius's goal was to manipulate his peers by planting the seed of fear that their prominent position in society and their livelihood were both at risk. He goaded them into action. After Demetrius planted the seeds of fear, doubt and anger in their minds, their hearts were infected and "they were filled with rage!" As the craftsmen erupted in anger, it created confusion and chaos so that a mob mentality emerged and those infected increased. Paul wanted to calm the growing agitation, but his friends, recognizing the volatility of the situation, restrained him. Once the crowd recognized Paul was a Jew (racism), it incited them further so that for two hours they yelled out, "Great is Artemis of the Ephesians." The problem is no one was questioning it. The people of the city were being led into an insane and unnecessary response.

Reread the story above, but consider it as present day. What do we see? Pride, jealousy, fear-mongering, racism, rage, mob violence and murderous intent. These responses are happening all around us as leaders and the media, filled with pride and jealousy for their positions, attempt to plant fear into a population to goad them into rage and action to a place of volatility, even murderous intent. Haven't we seen that in Washington, D.C., Seattle, Minneapolis, Portland and Illinois where fires, both emotional and physical, have been stoked with words to create a violent response? It is all part of the spiritual pandemic running rampant not only in America but around the world.

## THE ORIGIN OF PRIDE

The first act of pride was Lucifer's coup attempt in the heavenlies. As one of three archangels, he held a high position. This was the setup for the introduction of pride. He became full of himself, and the more he meditated on how great he was, the greater the infection grew within him until he was convinced of his own supremacy and determined that he would take over the Throne of Heaven. In his leadership role, he convinced one-third of the angels to join him.

**The first act of pride was Lucifer's coup attempt in the heavenlies.**

*"How you are fallen from heaven, O Day Star, son of Dawn! How you are cut down to the ground, you who laid the nations low! You said in your heart, 'I will ascend to heaven; above the stars of God; I will set my throne on high; I will sit on the mount of assembly in the far reaches of the north; I will*

*ascend above the heights of the clouds; I will make myself like the Most High.' But you are brought down to Sheol, to the far reaches of the pit."[7]*

We see this same spirit in the Prince of Tyre, which is the same spirit in the days of Ezekiel:

*The word of the Lord came to me: "Son of man, say to the prince of Tyre, Thus says the Lord God: 'Because your heart is proud, and you have said, "I am a god, I sit in the seat of the gods, in the heart of the seas," yet you are but a man, and no god, though you make your heart like the heart of a god—you are indeed wiser than Daniel; no secret is hidden from you; by your wisdom and your understanding you have made wealth for yourself, and have gathered gold and silver into your treasuries; by your great wisdom in your trade you have increased your wealth, and your heart has become proud in your wealth"'"* (Ezekiel 28:1-5 ESV).

It's important to recognize that this spirit continues to operate the same way as it did from its origins. Lucifer staged a coup d'état. What is happening in America right now? An attempted coup. Same spirit. Same action. Same virus.

When we become full of ourselves and allow pride to take root, the progression of the virus has begun. Pride is revealed when our thoughts are all about us. It is the big "I" rather than a heart submitted to God. It's important that we remember that *"God resists the proud, but gives grace to the humble."*[8] When we allow that seed to take root in our hearts, this is where the virus begins and the progression starts. Once that happens, we will find ourselves in a fight, not just against people, but ultimately against God.

One of my friends and fellow writer, Kim Potter, president of A New Thing Ministries, shared with me her thoughts on this subject.

"Someone asked me to write an article about pride. I have studied humility several times, and thought to myself *this should be easy.*

**When we become full of ourselves and allow pride to take root, the progression of the virus has begun**

"As I began to study, at first, I didn't find much that I hadn't already found when studying humility. That is, until I came upon an online article which listed the signs of pride in several different areas. I decided to print it off and study it. It was thirty-six pages long!

"One thing the author wrote that really opened my eyes was when he said, *'God had been resisting me. It was like His palm was firmly planted on my forehead as I walked through life and it was really uncomfortable. And it was constant. He doesn't body slam the proud, He just resists them.'*[9]

"The word 'resist' is defined in the *Webster's 1828 Dictionary* as 'to stand against. To oppose; strive against; defeat; frustrate; disappoint or interrupt progress.'[10]

"After reading this part of that article, I stopped. It was enlightening. It was illuminating. And it was convicting.

"I had to ask myself, 'In what areas of my life could God be resisting me?' I knew it was there; I just had to find out exactly where it was."

That is the question we should all stop right here to ask ourselves before moving ahead. Is God resisting us? If so, where? Are there any areas in our lives in which we feel continual push back, defeat, frustration or interrupted progress? Areas that we have attributed to a spiritual attack, in fact, may be resistance because we are operating in pride. And every single one of us has at one time or another been trapped in its web.

Proverbs tells us that *"Pride goes before destruction, and a haughty spirit before a fall."*[11]

This spirit of pride can be seen during the days of Jesus as He interacted with one particular group of spiritual leaders of his day—the Pharisees. Once we look at how this religious sect evolved, their susceptibility to pride becomes very clear.

According to the *Encyclopedia Britannica,* the Pharisees (Hebrew: *Perushim*) emerged as a distinct group shortly after the Maccabean revolt, about 165–160 BCE; they were, it is generally believed, spiritual descendants of the Hasideans. The Pharisees emerged as a party of laymen and scribes in contradistinction to the Sadducees—i.e., the party of the high priesthood that had traditionally provided the sole leadership of the Jewish people. The basic difference that led to the split between the Pharisees and the Sadducees lay in their respective attitudes toward the Torah (the first five books of the Bible) and the problem of finding in it answers to questions and bases for decisions about contemporary legal and religious matters arising under circumstances far different from those of the time of Moses. In their response to this problem, the Sadducees, on the one hand, refused to accept any precept as binding unless it was based directly on the Torah—i.e., the Written Law. The Pharisees, on the other hand, believed that the Law that God gave to Moses was twofold, consisting of the Written Law and the Oral Law—i.e., the teachings of the prophets and the oral traditions of the Jewish people. Whereas the priestly Sadducees taught that the written Torah was the only source of revelation, **the Pharisees admitted the principle of evolution in the Law: humans must use their reason in interpreting the Torah and applying it to contemporary problems.**

"Rather than blindly follow the letter of the Law even if it conflicted with reason or conscience, the Pharisees harmonized the teachings of the Torah with their own ideas or found their own ideas suggested or implied in it. They interpreted the Law according to its spirit. **When in the course of time a law had been outgrown or superseded by changing conditions, they gave it a new and more acceptable meaning, seeking scriptural support for their actions through a ramified system of hermeneutics.** It was because of this progressive tendency of the Pharisees that their interpretation of the Torah continued to develop and has remained a living force in Judaism."[12]

The way the Pharisees applied the Law is not really very different than what we see taking place in society today. It is how some churches or groups choose to reinterpret the Bible to make it more "applicable" to the day in which we live. Some feel we have outgrown the Bible or society has superseded it due to changing conditions. It is why the emergent church arose as people chose to reinterpret the Bible to fit their theology, rather than remain true to God's. Paraphrased, what is now promoted is a "progressive gospel" or theology adjusted to be socially acceptable to the day in which we live. In one sense, modern-day Pharisees.

Pharisees were completely convinced they were the wisest and only true God-appointed leaders. Yet, in their pride they were completely deceived.

How can we recognize the spirit of pride? By its destructive force.

*"Arrogant foes are attacking me, O God; ruthless people are trying to kill me—they have no regard for You."*[13]

Pride always seeks to destroy. Often coupled with jealousy, together the two forces seek to destroy people, relationships and hope. It becomes a consuming force. It is what currently fuels the attack against President Trump, as those determined to remove him from office are overtaken and blinded by the same spirit as the

Pharisees in days of old, convinced they are wiser, stronger, better. Convinced that they are "doing God's will" in their attempt to remove him from office. But is that truth or an indicator of the spiritual virus?

**The emergent church arose as people chose to reinterpret the Bible to fit their theology, rather than remain true to God's.**

It's important to recognize that it is impossible to reason with or try to speak logic to those who operate in this spirit. I often say, "Don't engage the rage." However, on social media I'm sometimes willing to enter into a discussion with people under the influence of this spirit when they comment on my page. Not because I expect to change their minds, but for the benefit of others reading the post to impart understanding and courage. This spirit seeks to intimidate and bully others into submission. We need to remember that greater is He who is in us. We don't run and cower from this spirit. Instead, we stand fast in truth and love. Light will always overcome the darkness.

When we see that destructive spirit of pride raise its head, our first response should be to pray for the individual that the blinders will be removed along with the spirit of pride. We must also pray and ask the Lord if we have embraced pride in any area unknowingly. Why? Because pride brings deception, and we must continually check our hearts to make sure *we* are not the ones who are deceived. When we see these issues in someone, we need to recognize that God reveals these to us first and foremost to pray rather than confront. This should always be our first step to eradicate the virus, but what happens if it progresses to stage two?

**This spirit seeks to intimidate and bully others into submission.**

## JEALOUSY

As already stated, jealousy almost always accompanies pride. Lucifer was jealous of God. In biblical history, Saul was jealous of David. Haman was jealous of Mordecai, and the Pharisees burned with jealousy against Jesus. He drew the crowds which they couldn't so they plotted to kill Him. Sounds similar to a certain presidential race at the moment, doesn't it? Consider Lucifer, Saul and Haman, who were all infected. What do they have in common? How it ended for them.

David encountered this spirit in King Saul after his many successes in battle which brought him to public attention. During a victory parade, after winning yet another battle, the women sang, *"Saul has slain his thousands, and David his tens of thousands."*[14] What leader wouldn't be jealous of such a chant? Saul's pride and jealousy were tweaked, and his relationship with David went downhill from there as the virus progressed.

There isn't a single person who hasn't dealt with pride. It is a devious foe. It silently enters our lives when we least expect it. A small success, some type of recognition or a pat on the back can send us to believe that we are something more than just a vessel for His glory. When we succumb to that subtle suggestion, we are ripe for deception. Everyone is susceptible. *"For false Christs and false prophets will arise and will show great signs and wonders, so as to mislead, if possible, even the elect."*[15]

Once the seeds of pride and jealousy have taken root, it is time for the second stage of the progression which is the entrance of the twins of offense and deception. Then like the Pharisees of old, we become Satan's tool to destroy others—including fellow believers. *"They will make you outcasts from the synagogue, but an hour is coming for everyone who kills you to think that he is offering service to God."*[16]

## There isn't a single person who hasn't dealt with pride.

It is the spirit in which a believer would turn over another believer to authorities and believe they are actually doing "God's work." That day is upon us. With the mounting fear of the corona virus, we see authorities give instruction for neighbors to report a neighbor if they aren't wearing a mask or not social distancing. On social media you can become a "fact checker" and report on someone with whom you disagree and have them put in "Facebook jail" without ever having to reveal your identity. It is the spirit in operation right now in our world.

This is a day when the body of Christ should unify as never before rather than launch offensives against each other. May we live as David did when he said, *"Search me, O God, and know my heart: try me, and know my thoughts: And see if there be any wicked way in me, and lead me in the way everlasting."*[17]

Once pride and jealousy have taken residence in their host, the next stage of the virus is inevitable. The entrance of twins.

Once pride and jealousy
have taken residence in their host,
the next stage of the virus is inevitable.
The entrance of twins.

# SCRIPTURES

*When pride comes, then comes disgrace, but with humility comes wisdom.* Proverbs 11:2

*In his arrogance the wicked man hunts down the weak,who are caught in the schemes he devises, He boasts about the cravings of his heart; he blesses the greedy and reviles the LORD. In his pride the wicked man does not seek him; in all his thoughts there is no room for God."* Psalm 10:2-4

*May the arrogant be put to shame for wronging me without cause, but I will meditate on your precepts.* Psalm 119:78

*The greedy stir up conflict, but those who trust in the Lord will prosper. Those who trust in themselves are fools, but those who walk in wisdom are kept safe.* Proverbs 28:25-26

*Whoever slanders their neighbor in secret, I will put to silence; whoever has haughty eyes and a proud heart, I will not tolerate.* Psalm 101:5

*But when his heart became arrogant and hardened with pride, he was deposed from his royal throne and stripped of his glory.* Daniel 5:20

*The pride of your heart has deceived you, you who live in the clefts of the rocks and make your home on the heights, you who say to yourself, 'Who can bring me down to the ground?'* Obadiah 1:3

*As it is, you boast in your arrogant schemes. All such boasting is evil.* James 4:16

*The Lord tears down the house of the proud, but he sets the widow's boundary stones in place.* Proverbs 15:25

*The arrogant dig pits to trap me, contrary to your law. All your commands are trustworthy; help me, for I am being persecuted without cause. They almost wiped me from the earth, but I have not forsaken your precepts.* Psalm 119:85-87

## Chapter 3

# OFFENSE:
# THE BLESSING BLOCKER

The next stage of the virus is offense. Offense is a blessing blocker. The problem is we often don't recognize when it has gained a foothold in our lives.

There have been numerous prophetic warnings to stay out of offense—especially this year, and with good reason. We need only turn on a news broadcast for the opportunity to take offense with something or someone. There is an ongoing attempt to pit young against old, white against black, male against female, rich against poor and the list goes on. It is a by-product of the virus, but also an intentional action from those intent on creating chaos and division.

43

This past year the Lord took me on a journey and opened my eyes to the indicators and subsequent damage of offense. "The greater the offense, the greater the deception," He spoke to me one day as I reviewed the many biblical examples of derailed lives. Cain, King Saul, Haman, the Pharisees, etc.

There are always warning signs, if we know what to look for. They are important indicators, which we need to heed, as we all have regular opportunities placed in our path daily to trap us in offense.

Offense often starts when a trigger is tripped. What are triggers? We all have them. They are created from painful experiences of our past or areas in which we have taken on the offense of others. They are unhealed wounds that have been buried. And like a field of land mines, anyone who walks through those fields will get blown up if they inadvertently stumble across the hidden mine or trigger.

Triggers not only release anger, but derail us as we then rabbit trail from the real issue at hand. One clear example occurred this past year in a discussion on my Facebook page during the COVID-19 outbreak. I posted a short article about how to recognize fake news by showing an example of a fake news story that had been published in my local paper. In the news account that was released, the media wrote about the first man in our city to die from COVID. However, as they shared the details of the story, they tweaked them slightly to illicit fear. The facts were that the man who passed had been a pastor in his younger years and was presently serving as a lay pastor/minister for his church. However, his full-time position was at a university in our city. Coworkers confirmed he had additional health issues prior to contracting COVID. I shared the facts and pointed out small things the media did to position the story in a way that would create a response of fear.

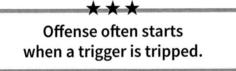

**Offense often starts
when a trigger is tripped.**

First, in their story they made it sound as if the man was the senior pastor of a church. Why? Because the undertones of that slight shift were subtle but real, "Even pastors aren't safe from this disease and can die." Next, they didn't reveal that there were comorbidity issues and other health problems already in the mix with the individual. They made it sound like he was completely healthy one day and dead two or three days later. It was not an honest account, but one intentionally meant to create fear. In my post, I simply tried to expose how the media tweaks the truth or withholds details to create a narrative. Boy, did it hit some triggers!

A distant family member of the deceased became enflamed with my comment that other health issues were involved and began cursing and name-calling me. He insisted there were no other issues, even though the man's coworkers verified discussions with the man over his health issues. Somehow this distant relative felt it dishonored his relative to bring up that he had additional health problems. The relative, now triggered, missed the point of the post and began a lengthy attack.

**Triggers not only release anger,
but derail us as we then rabbit trail
from the real issue at hand.**

Another friend was triggered because her father had been a lay minister, and she felt I was demeaning the fact that the man was no longer in full-time ministry. She felt I was saying that lay ministry was not as important. I never said or implied that, and it certainly was not my meaning. But her trigger was tripped as her father had at one time been a senior pastor and then in his later years a lay minister. So what she heard in her heart, because of the trigger, was that I was demeaning lay ministers. She too missed the entire point of the story which was how fake news is created. Instead she started a dialogue about the importance of lay ministers.

Another individual was triggered because they had battled their own numerous health concerns. She felt to mention that the man had battled with his health in many other areas was not respectful. She felt it necessary to criticize and correct my post.

Each of the individuals responded because something triggered within them from their past or personal history, which created an offense to which they felt they needed to respond. The trigger caused them to view the story from their personal filter which skewed the point. As they read, they lost sight of the actual purpose of the post, which was simply to explain how fake news happens. Their triggered emotions created the need to defend what they then perceived as the underdog. My intention was not to anger or demean anyone—certainly not the man who had passed who had spent his life serving the Lord. It simply stated facts from the story and how the media changed them slightly to create fear. All that was lost on those who became triggered. This is what happens when we read and hear things through the filter of our personal issues. If a trigger is present, suddenly anger can rear its ugly head. It is an indicator.

Whenever anger arouses in us, the first thing we need to ask ourselves is if we have a trigger that needs to be addressed. Even if the anger is motivated from a right heart, it may still be a root that needs to be pulled up. Otherwise it will continue to trigger us time and time again. It can affect our personal and professional lives.

A recent study conducted by Dr. Jeremy Berneth, a professor at San Diego State University, discovered that people who are easily offended make terrible employees because they never get anything done.

Berneth asked almost 400 employees, aged 25.9 on average, across seven U.S. colleges about different events that have recently gotten "substantial media attention."

The study notes that the events consisted of "17 items developed to assess the proclivity to be offended, 8 moral outrage items, 11 microaggression items and 9 political correctness items."

**People who are easily offended make terrible employees because they never get anything done.**

It noted that some people have a high "proclivity to be offended" (PTBO), which the study describes as "a state-like tendency to be sensitive to customarily innocuous societal events and traditions," for example "playing of the United States' National Anthem."

Those with a high PTBO showed a "tendency to view an array of events and/or traditions as offensive."

They also were "likely to feel that social events or traditions to which they take offense also violate moral or equitable standards," the study noted.

Basically, they're people who are easily triggered.

Dr Berneth found that high PTBOs are less productive, because they are constantly worrying about how the organization which they work for is "less fair" than everywhere else, and they "consume a lot of time complaining about trivial matters."[18]

America has become a land focused on offense and looking for it under every rock. News stories no longer just give us the news, but they have to share the color of skin of the individual or their education level, gender or sexual orientation. These become the basis from which they want us to view the story to trigger a sense of injustice. Now if skin color is an important part of a story, then we need to know it. If a true injustice has occurred, we want to know it. But when the story is about something else, and skin color, gender or sexual orientation is used to create offense, it is manipulation. We were created to desire justice. When we sense something is unjust, that sense of justice rises up within us to defend it. That is a good thing. Unfortunately, the media has abused that good nature within us to manipulate us with narratives where stories are not written from facts, but with an agenda to trigger.

Let's look at how America has become an offense-ridden land. Names of a sport's team or products such as syrup are now considered racial and offensive. Historical statues and names of roads are suddenly all under great scrutiny. How did we arrive at this place where everything has become an offense? It is all part of this virus which has become the true spiritual pandemic.

**How did we arrive at this place where everything has become an offense?**

## INDICATORS

While there are several signs which point to the possibility of offense in our hearts, one of the easiest to recognize is anger. It doesn't always mean there is offense. But it is a sign that there might be.

Anger is a natural response when our boundaries have been crossed. It is also a tool used by satan to manipulate and control us. Because most people will do anything to avoid confrontation, when someone in offense rises up in anger, the response of the average individual is to back away. This is what is happening right now. In fear of getting attacked, we slowly back away afraid to open our mouths regarding issues in which an offense laden, politically correct mantra has been strategically used to stir division and rage. As we read headlines or listen to the nightly propaganda rather than actual news stories, we are told what to think as inflammatory words are used to lead us to a conclusion. In an article from a true news journalist, the reader should never be able to tell which side the writer personally embraces. The story should provide facts alone which allow the reader to make their own determination of good or evil, guilty or not guilty. Those types of journalistic stories are rare today. Instead the "news" tells us how we are supposed to feel, what they deem as truth and what they want us to believe are "conspiracy theories." If we don't agree with their narratives and conclusions, we are belittled, demeaned and censored. This is the nature of offense.

It is so easy once you have encountered offense to take their offense, but the problem is once we allow that seed to incubate in our minds, a trigger is created and the lie becomes truth. It is one of the ways this virus can easily populate.

**Anger is a natural response
when our boundaries
have been crossed.**

During the early years of marriage, my husband and I lived in China and worked as English teachers. After our first year, we were asked by the teachers' organization that had placed us to be the leaders of our city team which consisted of approximately twenty American teachers. We were all there for the same purpose—to share the love of Christ.

Once we were made leaders, it triggered another couple on the team who were older, and who subsequently felt more qualified for the position. After our appointment, they worked relentlessly to discredit us and stir offense among the team. I didn't understand the virus at that point in my life or that they were infected. What we did realize was how angry they became over issues that shouldn't have been issues.

One day I came home from class and found a lengthy list of offenses taped to my door the couple felt we needed to correct immediately. They also gave us instructions on the list how we could approach them and when. We were only allowed to knock on their door at certain times of the day. We were not allowed to talk to their children. We were reprimanded for talking in the stairwell. We were told our leadership was pathetic and ineffective. We were reprimanded that the class schedule we had received from the school was not to their liking and was somehow our fault. On and on the list went with their frustrations and demands. My initial response was to take offense at their offense! Anger rose up within me at their unfair and petty accusations. But immediately the Holy Spirit spoke to my heart, "Forgive."

That's not what I wanted to do in that moment, but I pushed away the offense and began to pray. I thanked God for the couple and asked Him to bless them. After several minutes, my heart calmed and I began to write a response to their note. Instead of defending myself, I accepted all their criticism and apologized for every single thing on their list without reservation. Every. Single. Area. No matter how ridiculous their claims, I simply apologized.

## My initial response was to take offense at their offense!

I then went to their apartment, which was right across from us, and taped my response to their door, since I was not allowed to knock on the door. I then went back into our apartment and went about my day, free of the offense that tried to deposit on me. What happened next is a testimony to the power of forgiveness.

That evening the couple knocked on our door. With slight apprehension we invited them in wondering if the floodgates of anger were about to unleash once again. Instead the woman began to cry. "I'm so sorry," she began. Healing took place that night between us as the two repented for their harsh words, criticism and accusations against us. It was a wonderful moment. Unfortunately, it didn't last long. For when a trigger is present, if it is not uprooted, it will return full force with all its emotional minions.

Within three days the woman was bad-mouthing us and criticizing us again to the group and to the Chinese students and officials. Her rage knew no bounds as she unleashed her fury. Unfortunately, the root of pride and jealousy had not been removed when we prayed together three days before. Not only were they still infected, but the virus had progressed at an unbelievable rate.

Attacks can come from people we don't know as well.

Recently, I had an individual I didn't know attack me on social media because they had taken offense over the fact I had not responded to a private message they had sent me. Evidently I had agreed to lead a segment of a prayer call for their ministry. However, after I requested information on how to connect and what time I was supposed to be involved, communication fell apart. I never heard back from them, evidently missing their response which came as a private message. I often miss private messages as I receive hundreds every day. Because I never saw his response, I missed the prayer call. The ministry leader never e-mailed or contacted me any other way, and it didn't register with me that I had never received the additional information needed to participate. Five weeks later the individual came onto my Facebook page to call me out. When confronted, I apologized for missing the event and explained I never saw his response giving me the additional details.

In most cases that would solve an issue. But not here, which is the indicator that something is amiss. Even after apologizing, he continued to post his anger and judgment against me at how I had acted. He called me a liar. He claimed I broke my promise. He told me I was following Jesus only with my mouth, but not my heart. His offense continued to pour out even after I blocked him on Facebook. Next, he came after me via e-mail. "What would Jesus do if in my place?" he concluded.

Well, not what he was doing I was sure. In his offense he felt he was obligated to correct me publicly. But the Bible is very clear on how we can remain out of offense. It is by dealing with issues directly and privately with the individual. We find the solution in Matthew 18:15-17:

> *"If your brother or sister sins, go and point out their fault, just between the two of you. If they listen to you, you have won them over. But if they will not listen, take one or two others along, so that 'every matter may be established by the testimony of two or three witnesses.' If they still refuse to listen, tell it to the church; and if they refuse to listen even to the church, treat them as you would a pagan or a tax collector."*

The correct response when an issue of disagreement or hurt occurs is to first take it to the Lord. Forgive. Let it go if it is something that does not require a deeper level of resolution. If you can't let it go, then biblical conflict resolution requires we first go directly to the individual to discuss the hurt, confusion, question or injustice. If that doesn't work, take someone with you to discuss the conflict and help moderate. If that doesn't work, only then are we to bring it out into the public—to the church. However, even then it's important to remember how Jesus treated tax collectors.

When the ministry leader went straight to number three to "call me out" publicly and try to shame me for missing his event, my apology did nothing to assuage his offense and rage. He was caught in the virus and didn't even realize it was guiding his actions and emotions. The problem is that now infected, the virus will continue to operate in his life and flavor and poison every aspect of the ministry he runs until it destroys both him and the ministry unless he receives the cure. Without it, the virus always leads to death.

How can this be seen in our lives? Think about the times you have been angered over an injustice. Injustice *should* create anger. Jesus showed anger when the temple was turned into a marketplace and responded accordingly. But here's the difference. While Jesus responded to the action (spirit), He did not hold offense at the people behind the action. He responded to the spirit and called out the action, but He didn't attack the people.

Jesus often called out the Pharisees. He even called them "dogs" and "vipers." I mentioned this to a group in which I once took part. They were enraged that President Trump had referred to the members of the murderous MS-13 gang as "dogs." They insisted no one should ever be referred to as an animal. When I reminded them that Jesus did that very thing on certain occasions, they told me that the scripture didn't apply! This also is an indicator of offense when we pick and choose what scriptures apply and what doesn't to support what we want to believe. I have had a few occasions in which a believer blew up in rage as we were in a discussion over a disagreement after I shared a scripture in response. That is an immediate red flag that the individual is caught in the virus. Offense tricks us into believing we are operating for a just cause, when actually we are operating out of a religious spirit as offense blinds us to truth.

**He responded to the spirit
and called out the action,
but He didn't attack the people.**

When we feel a "righteous anger" against injustice arise in our hearts, we want to stand up and defend the underdog, right? But this is where we must be very cautious. Because offense can mirror righteous anger and then it is very easy to become angry at the "opposing side" who we feel created the injustice. For example, when we see injustice toward the poor, it is easy to take offense at the rich. When we see injustice toward a minority group, it is easy to take offense at the majority group. When this happens, when we take on the injustice in our heart, then we have opened the door to offense. It's that simple. It becomes our choice if we walk through that door. How can we avoid offense? We have to *"keep our hearts with all diligence for out of it spring the issues of life."*[19] This is a key.

If we don't guard our heart, we can be easily manipulated to become activists who then target *those people* rather than the spirit behind the injustice. We can then become almost hyper vigilant against the injustice and thus can actually become part of the problem. Why? Because offense has entered the picture without our realizing it. And this is where we see offense's twin—deception.

**If we don't guard our heart, we can be easily manipulated to become activists who then target *those people*.**

## DECEPTION

The social justice movement in America stems from this issue. It is a deception that causes us to believe we are actually working from a "righteous" standpoint to obtain justice. But it isn't biblical justice. It is the antithesis of biblical justice. It is rooted in pride and offense that pits one group against another.

The key to remember is that our battle is never against flesh and blood. *"For our struggle is not against flesh and blood, but against the rulers, against the authorities, against the powers of this dark world and against the spiritual forces of evil in the heavenly realms."*[20]

There is an unholy progression that can be traced biblically over and over again in the areas of deception and offense. This spiritual progression can be seen in the life of Saul (or the Pharisees in the New Testament) as he walks through each step of the spiritual virus which starts with pride/jealousy. As you read the story below from 1 Samuel 18, watch the progression and indicators that follow: offense, deception, anger which evolves to rage and murderous intent. Then once it hits a final tipping point, it reaches the last stage of the progression—insanity.

In the beginning when Saul was chosen to be king, we don't see pride. Instead, we see a man who hid himself in a haystack completely unconfident of who he was or how God could use him! Yet once he was established as king, his confidence grew along with pride in his position until he was infected by the virus. Eventually he succumbed to each stage of the progression:

1. Saul became angry when David was honored above himself (1 Samuel 18:6-9). **(pride/jealousy)**

2. He took offense at the praise David received (1 Samuel 18:7). **(offense)**

3. He rose up in anger and hurled a spear at his own son (1 Samuel 20:30-33). **(anger/rage)**

4. He believed God was helping him to find David so that he could kill him (1 Samuel 23:7). **(deception)**

5. He spent more time chasing after David to kill him then taking care of the kingdom (1 Samuel 24). **(murderous intent)**

6. After Saul turned from the Lord, his mind snapped. Until his death he lived in rage, fear and torment until in desperation he sought insight from a witch who accurately prophesied his death (1 Samuel 28). **(insanity)**

7. Ultimately, Saul lost his kingdom and his life (1 Samuel 31 and 2 Samuel 3:10). **(death)**

After pride enters, it always births the twins of offense and deception. They go hand in hand. I believe that is why this word to avoid offense is so important. For if we take offense, we have then opened the door to deception which then blinds us from the ability to see that we are actually the issue and in error. It can change a person of virtue into someone else entirely.

**After pride enters, it always births the twins of offense and deception.**

Have you ever watched as someone you respected or knew well began to behave in ways not only untypical, but were, in fact, ungodly and prideful? Instead of acting with kindness and honor, angry, pride-filled accusations spew from their mouth. It is like the man who came against me on Facebook. I'm sure he was a good man. But once his pride was wounded that I had not joined his prayer call, offense came in along with deception, that he felt it was the right thing to do to shame me publicly for missing the call. Actions such as these are all indicators of the virus's progression.

A present-day illustration of this progression, in my opinion, is seen in the life of Senator John McCain.

(Please don't get offended by that statement. I want to use what happened publicly between him and President Trump to illustrate the progression of the virus.)

Many will remember that McCain ran for president along with numerous others for the 2016 bid. During an interview, then candidate Trump made the statement that Senator McCain was not a war hero.[21] I'm not here to defend or discuss that statement. What we are looking at is how this tweaked John McCain's **pride.** Understandable. But he had a choice to let it go or allow offense to root into the soil of his heart which is exactly what happened. We can watch the tragic events that followed as he became infected. After he didn't get elected president, **jealousy** toward President Trump (which remember often follows pride) entered. By his own admission he was **offended** over critical words Donald Trump said about him during the presidential debates. This is where I believe deception entered the picture. What is clear is he made the decision to turn against his own Party and began to work against Trump who was now president-elect. I believe in his mind he was convinced he was doing a good thing **(deception)** as he secretly released classified documents to the FBI to try to remove Trump from office even before he had been inaugurated.[22] His pride made him a pawn. He became **enraged** at President Trump and seemed to make it his final mission in life, after the diagnosis of a brain tumor, to see President Trump fail. Of the senator's perplexing actions to side with Democrats the final months of his life, Corey Jones, a state director for the New Right, a political organization focused on uniting conservatives supportive of Trump's "America First" agenda, stated:

"I think McCain comes off as a very bitter individual. Instead of leaving the past in the past, McCain has made it a mission of his to undermine the Trump agenda. Trump made some strong remarks toward Senator McCain during the election, and McCain can't seem to move on."[23]

In the final months of McCain's life, we see a **murderous** intent against President Trump's reputation and position determined to see him removed at all cost **(insanity)** as he shifts from Republican to Democrat to see his political rival destroyed. As the brain tumor consumed McCain, so did the virus; and he died still shaking his fist in the air at the president as seen in the song he chose for his funeral, "I Did It My Way."[24] It was a confirmation of the pride that had consumed him and controlled his actions even to his death. As we continue to follow the progress of the virus, make no mistake, it always leads to the death of its host.

It is essential that we pay attention and watch for these indicators of offense and deception in our lives. Offense not only leads us down a dangerous road, but it blocks the blessings that we receive when we are rightly related to others. Sometimes it is the very people we get offended with who hold the breakthrough to our blessing. God often places it in our lives as a test.

## As the brain tumor consumed McCain, so did the virus.

I worked with an individual a few years ago who was praying for financial breakthrough. Unfortunately, they became infected with this virus as I hit a trigger in their life and they blew up in anger. No matter how hard I tried to reconcile with them, it was to no avail and they ended the relationship with the words, "I refuse to work with you."

In severing the relationship, they also severed the financial blessing for which they prayed. I shook my head in disbelief as I added up the financial cost to their business. It was between $75,000 and $100,000 from projects they would have received had we remained in relationship doing business together. The very thing for which they prayed, they refused once they were infected with the virus. Offense became the blessing blocker, and they had no idea they were the ones who had stopped the blessing. The virus will extract a hefty toll on our lives, and deception will keep us from recognizing it.

Each day we have a decision to make as the opportunity for offense arises over present-day issues—such as the corona virus. One group is offended at those who don't wear masks believing it is uncaring and unchristian, while the other group is offended at those who do wear masks believing they aren't walking in faith but in fear. It doesn't matter if either is right. The root of pride is at the core, and the infection from pride and offense is the same.

We see the same thing regarding the politically charged offense surrounding the Black Lives Matter movement. I've heard many people respond regarding the slogan as they state, "Black lives *do* matter, but *all* lives matter." One woman responded to that comment, "Then you have no idea how that hurts me and shows me that black lives *don't* matter to you." How did she hear that? But that is the point of deception. You hear something completely different than what was said. So even though the comment "all lives matter" was prefaced with "black lives *do* matter," all the young woman heard was black lives *don't* matter. But in reality, the bigger lie she believed was *her* life didn't matter.

That is the danger of offense and deception. It clouds what we hear as words are filtered through the lens of deception. Take any issue and you will always find some people for it and others against it. And when that occurs, we have a choice to make. Will we take up offense with those whom we disagree and allow the infection to progress in our hearts? Or will we make the decision to lay down our right to be offended, forgive and discuss the issue at hand? Our decision will determine whether we fall into that deadly trap of the progression or recognize it for what it is.

How do we protect ourselves from that trap?

*"Get rid of all bitterness, rage and anger, brawling and slander, along with every form of malice. Be kind and compassionate to one another, forgiving each other, just as in Christ God forgave you."*[25]

It's really a simple solution. We must *daily* guard our hearts against taking the bait of offense which opens the door to deception. Because once we believe the deceptive lie, from that point, redemption requires a miraculous intervention.

# Scriptures

*A person's wisdom yields patience; it is to one's glory to overlook an offense.* (Proverbs 19:11)

*A brother offended is harder to be won than a strong city, and contentions are like the bars of a citadel.* (Proverbs 18:19 NASB)

*And "A stone of stumbling, and a rock of offense." They stumble because they disobey the word, as they were destined to do.* (1 Peter 2:8 ESV).

*Bearing with one another, and forgiving each other, whoever has a complaint (offense) against anyone; just as the Lord forgave you, so also should you.* (Colossians 3:13 NASB)

*Hatred stirs up strife, but love covers all offenses.* (Proverbs 10:12 ESV)

*Whoever covers an offense seeks love, but he who repeats a matter separates close friends.* (Proverbs 17:9 ESV)

*Great peace have they which love thy law: and nothing shall offend them.* (Psalm 119:165 KJV)

*Even if they sin against you seven times in a day and seven times come back to you saying 'I repent,' you must forgive them.* (Luke 17:4)

*[Love] does not dishonor others, it is not self-seeking, it is not easily angered, it keeps no record of wrongs.* (1 Corinthians 13:5)

*And when you stand praying, if you hold anything against anyone, forgive them, so that your Father in heaven may forgive you your sins.* (Mark 11:25)

## Chapter 4

# THE DECEPTION
# OF DECEPTION

Years ago, my husband and I encountered a tragic situation that reveals the nature and danger of deception. As I mentioned in the previous chapter, my husband and I lived and worked in China as English teachers in the early years of marriage. After the first year, we enrolled in a language school to learn Mandarin. After four years of hard work, we held a pretty moderate grasp of the language.

Each Saturday I met with several female Chinese students who had become close friends. We cooked lunch together, talked and then studied the Bible together. However, one Saturday when I arrived after I walked in the door, I saw an Asian looking man already teaching the girls. I had no idea who he was or why he was there.

"Karen, this is Brother Zhu," one of the ladies whispered as she pointed me to a seat. "He is an anointed prophet from Taiwan. He has been teaching us all week. We were sure you wouldn't mind if he took your session with us today."

I wasn't sure what to say, but it appeared the decision had already been made. So I sat down in the back to listen. Zhu spoke fast and with a thick accent quite different from the Chinese accent I was used to, so following him in a second language was difficult. Yet things he said began to jump out at me.

"Except for Jesus, I'm the only one who has ever fasted forty days and received such revelation."

"God has anointed me to come and teach you the truth and correct your error."

"I am a prophet and highly anointed of God. You must listen to me."

Could I have heard the man right? Part of me wanted to jump up and put an end to his prideful message, but because Mandarin was a second language, I had to be sure I wasn't just jumping to conclusions.

Turns out I wasn't.

After the meeting I talked with the ladies in attendance to confirm if I had heard correctly. I had. Returning home that afternoon I discussed my concerns with my husband. We prayed together and asked the Lord what we should do next. We were young leaders and had never dealt with this type of situation before. We chose to approach Mr. Zhu and his wife according to Matthew 18:18. This is the biblical passage on conflict resolution which I mentioned earlier. It instructs us to first go to the person directly. If they won't listen, take someone with you. If they still won't listen, we are to take it to the church. Because of the language difference, we took a mature Chinese believer who was also skilled in English to go with us to translate. We wanted to ensure that communications didn't go awry.

However, Mr. Zhu and his wife were combative from the beginning. They didn't want to discuss the areas in scripture they had tweaked to fit their theology. Zhu insisted that God had personally given him revelation which superseded scripture. He and his wife exploded in anger and began to criticize and name call us. Offended that we questioned them, they immediately went to the Chinese believers to denounce us and warn them to never meet with us again. Manipulation and control (witchcraft) manifested as they worked to remove us from a place of leadership among the Chinese believers.

Unfortunately, the Chinese Christians in our area weren't the only ones who had fallen under Mr. Zhu's spell. Some of the other missionaries in our group (perhaps they couldn't understand him because of the language barrier?) had jumped on his band wagon extolling his "anointing." As is often the case, they confused charisma with anointing. My husband, Kevin, and I were waving red flags of concern. This self-proclaimed "prophet" was pouring out erroneous teachings that did not align with scripture. It contained just enough of the Word to tickle the ears, but otherwise was all about exalting him and his message. It was pure deception.

**They immediately went to the Chinese believers to denounce us and warn them to never meet with us again.**

We tried to meet with the man and his wife again. It didn't last long. Eventually they refused to listen or talk with us further and began to "prophesy" to the group about us. One would give a "tongue" and the other an "interpretation" which was always something to the affect that Kevin and I were evil and leading the group astray. He told them God had revealed to him that He was displeased with us. He issued warnings that if any in the group continued to associate with us, they would come to great harm.

The indicators of the spiritual virus could easily be seen: pride, jealousy, offense, deception, anger/rage . . . Unfortunately, we didn't have the revelation of the virus at that time. All we knew was a supposed brother in the Lord had come into our city and was now working to divide the church.

With great dismay, I watched as the Chinese community of believers that we had loved and worked with for the past five years began to splinter as they took sides over what to do with this man. Some believed his words that he was a "prophet of God." Others trusted the fruit and long relationship we had developed with them over the previous years. In the end the church split as some refused to fellowship with those that maintained their friendship with Kevin and me. Eventually the "prophet" and his wife left the city, but the damage they had done remained. The group remained divided. The virus and the pride and offense he planted began to infect many.

The progression of this virus always seeks to remove, silence and destroy. Its goal is to take over, control and manipulate. This is the spirit of the world today that has tried to permeate the Church and the government. It comes in the form of pride and self-revelation and seeks to divide and destroy the unity of the believers. It seeks out those who are not firmly planted in the Word of God as it speaks snippets of the Word that "tickle the ears," but in reality, deceives. Satan often uses that trick. In the wilderness he tossed scripture at Jesus as a weapon. He tried to dangle position before Jesus, which is what would have motivated Satan, but it held no lure for the Son of Man. He knew who He was and would not take the bait. Instead, Jesus used the Word to counter satan's deceptive lie.

> *"The devil led him up to a high place and showed him in an instant all the kingdoms of the world. And he said to him, 'I will give you all their authority and splendor; it has been given to me, and I can give it to anyone I want to. If you worship me, it will all be yours.'*
>
> *Jesus answered, "It is written: 'Worship the Lord your God and serve him only.'"*[26]
>
> *"Then the devil took Him into the holy city and had Him stand on the pinnacle of the temple, and said*

*to Him, 'If You are the Son of God, throw Yourself down; for it is written,*

*"He will command His angels concerning You"; and "On their hands they will bear You up, so that You will not strike Your foot against a stone."*

*Jesus said to him, "On the other hand, it is written, 'You shall not put the Lord your God to the test.'"*[27]

How do we inoculate ourselves from this virus? How do we recognize its presence? The key to avoid deception is as Jesus did. We are to keep our feet firmly planted in the Word of God. We must constantly keep ourselves humble before the Lord (removing pride) and refuse offense.

Over confidence, reliance upon charisma and false humility are all areas which can denote pride, but are easily missed as we look at our own lives. Actions are indicators. It is important we keep on the watch for the other indicators of the progression such as offense and anger especially in our own lives. Remember, all that glitters is not gold. We live in a day when we cannot afford to be deceived by "signs," but instead must be able to recognize and know Truth.

No matter how grounded we are in the Word, if we allow pride/jealousy and offense to take root in our heart, it will open the door to deception. When that happens, we can't hear or see accurately. We think we can, but we can't.

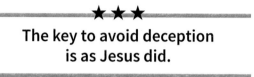

**The key to avoid deception
is as Jesus did.**

This is how believers—even strong believers—think they could never be deceived and are then carried away by the winds of deception. And what's worse? They don't even recognize it. We have all seen where well-recognized and anointed ministers, who may be accurate in most areas of their lives, begin to preach a new doctrine based on areas of idolatry or offense. When social justice (which is when our hearts are stirred and we are encouraged to take up an offense) takes precedence over scripture (biblical justice), that is a sure sign that offense has taken root and the individual has been infected by this spiritual virus. When this enters a church, it causes it to splinter and divide which then diminishes our strength as we fight among ourselves.

The nature of the spirit of deception is when we are deceived, we can't see it. That is how we can all easily fall prey to this insidious control. How do we break free? By *daily* praying and asking the Holy Spirit to reveal any area in which we aren't seeing clearly.

In 2015 when Donald Trump hit the national scene as a presidential candidate, like many, I laughed. What did he think he was doing? But then as he started filling auditoriums to capacity with his rallies, I got mad. Couldn't people see who he was? I was blown up over his past womanizing, his verbal name-calling, his arrogance. I went from laughing to anger. When my mom tried to talk to me about him, I remember raising my hand to stop her, "I don't want to hear it, Mom," I instructed.

For the record I didn't vote for him in the primaries. But it was what happened afterward that got my attention. After the primary, Dr. Ben Carson, whom I highly respected, came out and endorsed Donald Trump for president. What? I was shocked. But it was the letter Dr. Carson wrote and the qualities he championed in Mr. Trump that left me speechless. He referred to him as humble. Gracious. Caring. Godly. Okay, I didn't see any of those characteristics at the time in Donald Trump. I shook my head as I humbled my heart and prayed, "Lord, help me to see whatever I'm missing."

"Then you have to shut up," He immediately responded to my invitation.

So I did. I chose to quit bad-mouthing Trump, and instead pray and watch. It didn't happen overnight, but over the next two to three months it was as if a veil lifted off my eyes. Once I quit bad-mouthing and attacking the man and instead began to pray for him, I started seeing qualities that had been completely hidden. Like many, I had listened to the media and then almost daily would be blown up in offense. Now I took those areas of offense and simply prayed. And the transformation that happened in my heart and head was nothing short of miraculous. I didn't ask to like Trump. I never expected to, but God changed my heart. That's what prayer can do when we pray for our hearts to align with God's heart and we are willing to pray for those in leadership with whom we disagree.

**I shook my head as I humbled my heart and prayed, "Lord, help me to see whatever I'm missing."**

The offense and anger I had toward Donald Trump dissipated and with it the deception that had kept me blinded to the qualities Dr. Carson had seen, but I couldn't. That's what deception does. It keeps us focused on the offense and unable to see anything that would challenge the narrative we believe.

An obvious area in which deception has reigned in America is in the area of abortion. I've watched in amazement as good people rally around the "right" to murder the unborn and stand with Planned Parenthood even as those same individuals claim they stand with Christ. But the two cannot coexist. It is deception. What many of those supporting abortion don't realize in their deception is that Margaret Sanger, founder of Planned Parenthood, was blatantly racist. She boldly stated her goal when she said of blacks, immigrants and indigents, "They are, 'human weeds,' 'reckless breeders,' 'spawning . . . human beings' who never should have been born."[28] Sanger had a goal to eliminate the black race via abortion and yet is applauded as a hero. Yet her goal to eliminate the black race has been very successful as black women freely march into her facilities to abort their children.

According to a report in the *Wall Street Journal,* there is an "outsize toll that abortion has taken on the black population post-*Roe*. In New York City, thousands more black babies are aborted than born alive each year, and the abortion rate among black mothers is more than three times higher than it is for white mothers. According to a city Health Department report released in May, between 2012 and 2016 black mothers terminated

136,426 pregnancies and gave birth to 118,127 babies. By contrast, births far surpassed abortions among whites, Asians and Hispanics."[29]

The tragedy of the deception promoted as "our right" is that the last several years the black population has been reduced by almost 1 percent each year. If this continues, Sanger will have achieved her goal with the help of the very people she despised. *That* is deception.

Stay with me, because some will stop reading right here either in offense because you are one who supports abortion or because you think, "Well, that is not me." But that is exactly the thought deception creates. For the deceptive nature of the spirit of deception is that we don't recognize we are deceived. I mean, that's the point, right?

I was in a small prayer meeting one time and we were talking about the danger of deception when one of the participants spoke up and said, "I can't be deceived." My head jerked up as I heard the spirit of pride and deception leave her mouth. I couldn't believe it. "Anyone can be deceived," I responded gently.

"I can't," she replied. "I was at one time and I recognized it and so I can no longer be deceived."

And yet she was right in the middle of it.

When we think, "I'm not deceived," or "I can't be deceived," we need to retrace our steps. First Timothy 4:1 NASB says, *"But the Spirit explicitly says that in later times some will fall away from the faith, paying attention to deceitful spirits and doctrines of demons."* We all can be deceived. No one is exempt. When we think we can't be, we are actually already there. The only way to avoid deception is to take the following steps:

1. Stay in the Word of God.

2. Guard your heart with all diligence. Do not allow offense to take hold.

3. Humble yourself before the Lord, and daily ask Him to remove any area of pride that may have found a foothold.

4. Ask the Holy Spirit to reveal if there is any area of pride, offense or deception operating in your life.

**The deceptive nature of the spirit of deception is that we don't recognize we are deceived. I mean, that's the point, right?**

It is only once we have humbled ourselves before the Lord that deception can be eradicated and revealed. It is not something we can do or recognize on our own. It is a spiritual issue and must be addressed with a spiritual solution. Only then can we stop the progression before it goes to the next indicator which has erupted in violence across our land.

# SCRIPTURES

*I urge you, brothers and sisters, to watch out for those who cause divisions and put obstacles in your way that are contrary to the teaching you have learned. Keep away from them. For such people are not serving our Lord Christ, but their own appetites. By smooth talk and flattery they deceive the minds of naive people.* (Romans 16:17-18)

*Like a maniac shooting flaming arrows of death is one who deceives their neighbor and says, "I was only joking!"* (Proverbs 26:18-19)

*Charm is deceptive, and beauty is fleeting; but a woman who fears the Lord is to be praised.* (Proverbs 31:30)

*Then you will be handed over to be persecuted and put to death, and you will be hated by all nations because of me. At that time many will turn away from the faith and will betray and hate each other, and many false prophets will appear and deceive many people.* (Matthew 24:9-11)

*But encourage one another daily, as long as it is called "Today," so that none of you may be hardened by sin's deceitfulness.* (Hebrews 3:13)

*The wisdom of the prudent is to give thought to their ways, but the folly of fools is deception.* (Proverbs 14:8)

*Don't let anyone deceive you in any way, for that day will not come until the rebellion occurs and the man of lawlessness is revealed, the man doomed to destruction.* (2 Thessalonians 2:3)

*Do not deceive yourselves. If any of you think you are wise by the standards of this age, you should become "fools" so that you may become wise.* (1 Corinthians 3:18)

*Indeed, all who desire to live godly in Christ Jesus will be persecuted. But evil men and impostors will proceed from bad to worse, deceiving and being deceived.* (2 Timothy 3:12-13 NASB)

*If anyone thinks they are something when they are not, they deceive themselves.* (Galatians 6:3)

*But prove yourselves doers of the word, and not merely hearers who delude themselves.* (James 1:22 NASB)

## Chapter 5

# WHEN ANGER TURNS TO RAGE

Anger is an acid that can do more harm
to the vessel in which it is stored than
to anything on which it is poured.[30]
—Mark Twain, American writer

Sitting across from my client, we had been going over an upcoming project. Seconds before he had high-fived me on an accomplishment, yet now I watched as his eyes narrowed. He lowered his head refusing to make further eye contact. I had seen that look before, and my stomach knotted in anticipation of the outburst I knew from experience was about to be unleashed.

My mind swirled as I reviewed the last few sentences of our conversation. What on earth could have caused such a complete and dramatic shift in emotions? From my vantage point there had been nothing out of the ordinary, aggressive or critical in the conversation, and yet his rage exploded. That's when I recognized it was a trigger. I had inadvertently stumbled across a hidden land mine and the explosion that resulted left me bruised and bloodied. The problem was, I had no idea what I'd hit so I could avoid it in the future.

Angry outbursts are becoming more the norm than the exception. Common courtesy and kindness are in short supply as we believe "our rights" somehow are more important than that of those around us. My son and I were going through a fast-food drive through a couple of years ago when an older gentleman driving a very expensive sports car just ahead of us unloaded two to three fast food sacks of trash on the ground at the menu board after he ordered. Completing his order, he drove ahead to the pick-up window. After I drove up to place our order, I turned to my teenage son. "Honey, can you get out of the car and pick up that man's trash, please." After we ordered, I pulled up behind "Mr. Trash" to wait our turn. Putting the car in park, I grabbed the trash he had unloaded and walked up to the pick-up window. Handing the garbage to the cashier I said, "This man dropped his trash at the order window. I'm sure it was an accident. Can you put it in the garbage, please?" I handed over the sacks and walked back to my car with no interaction with the man in the car. After receiving his food purchase, "Mr. Trash" drove around the restaurant, pulled up to us and started pelting my car with more trash he had with him. Then he sped off laughing. If he had been a teenager it would have been easier to excuse his juvenile behavior. He wasn't. I would guess he was in his late sixties or seventies and obviously well-off financially based on the high-end sports car he drove. Yet childish rage controlled him.

## I had inadvertently stumbled across a hidden land mine

Most people will do anything to avoid that kind of rage or conflict. My action to pick up the man's trash and hand it to the cashier in front of him was something probably ninety percent of people would never do. I get that. However, statistics reveal that in society today, most people will do just about anything to avoid anger or conflict. When we know we are around a person given to rage, most of us turn our heads and tiptoe away afraid of setting off their wrath. Unfortunately, the result is now a world full of self-entitled, "me first" individuals who believe *their* rights matter but *ours* don't. Conflict avoidance gets us nowhere. It only empowers juvenile behavior. It is why we are to discipline our children as they grow up. Why we have rules. Why we shouldn't ignore anger, but rather work to remove it and de-escalate it.

But what happens when *we* are the ones triggered in anger?

How many times have you read a Facebook post, a tweet, a news story that so angered you that your immediate response was to hit "unfriend," "block" or "delete"? I'm not saying there aren't times to use those tools. There certainly are. But are we *reacting* in anger or are we waiting until we take a deep breath, contemplate and then operate out of a thoughtful response?

*"'In your anger do not sin': Do not let the sun go down while you are still angry"*[31] is important advice that we all should remember. Anger will happen. What we do with it is what matters.

Several years ago, I was part of a community group with numerous other families in which we all had school-aged kids. That was the common thread of our community. We did life together as we watched our kids grow. We organized field trips and activities for our kids together. We did birthday parties. We sat around the pool together over the summer as our kids splashed and played.

That is until there was conflict.

## Anger will happen.
## What we do with it is what matters.

A place of disagreement on how the community should be organized resulted in flared anger. Eventually one of the leaders of the group made the decision to leave and start her own group—taking many in the current community with her. Rather than staying to work through to a place of resolution, she positioned herself as the victim and effectively split the group in half. Friendships were ripped apart. Families once in community were now excommunicated by the split as the new group would have nothing to do with the previous group. That anger and disagreement among the parents then filtered into the kids. Not only did the adults lose relationship, but life-long friendships among our kids were destroyed.

Fast forward almost ten years later and some of those friends who left have now reached back out to restore relationship. The tragedy is that although the hurts and wounds of the actions years ago are now a distant memory, the season of those friendships has passed. Our kids are now grown. We don't attend the same church or functions. We no longer have the same interests. Try as I may, I could find no place to reconnect with some of these friends from years past. The relationships were lost. Sadly, the anger and offense that split our group completely changed the outcome of those friendships forever.

When we respond with anger rather than trying to resolve issues, broken relationships will almost always be the outcome. Some people can look back over their lives and see a path littered with broken relationships. Consider some of those relationships now. Can you see the progression of the virus in play either in yourself or the other individual? Pride, jealousy, offense, deception . . . anger.

And when anger is left unchecked, it will turn to rage.

## RAGE: THE BATTLE AGAINST RECONCILIATION

It's hard to go through a day without encountering rage in some fashion. Road rage. Economic rage. Political rage. Rage over religious or moral differences, and I'm not talking just anger, but rage that explodes on the scene in unjustifiable proportion that leaves us shaking our head. But make no mistake, it is a warning sign of a greater issue at play that must be uprooted and prayed out.

There are numerous biblical examples of this, one of the clearest between King Saul and David. (If you are unfamiliar with the account of King Saul and David from biblical history you can read 1 Samuel chapters 15-31.)

At first King Saul was grateful for David as the young man played his harp to sooth Saul's turbulent emotions. But after David killed Goliath and garnered success after success, Saul became jealous which then led to offense. Now wrapped in offense, his thinking was no longer clear. (Note: Discernment that may serve us well in normal times is reduced to suspicion and is perverted when we have an issue with someone that becomes offense. This was the case of Saul.) This is where we encounter the next step in the progression because offense always brings its twin—deception.

Saul was deceived. He believed David was out to steal the throne and in fear, he became enraged. Saul in a very short time progressed from jealousy, to offense, to deception, then to anger and rage. Have you ever encountered this with someone? Where a relatively normal conversation suddenly erupted into not just anger, but rage? Perhaps the individual just had a bad day. Certainly that can happen. No harm, no foul. But it can also be an indicator that there are other issues under the surface.

We see this all around us in the world today with uncertainty how to address it. And there lies another problem. When we try to deal with rage, we are actually only dealing with a symptom. What we must get to is the root—pride. If the root is not removed, the issue will return.

Rage was introduced in the relationship between Saul and David because of the fault line of pride. Saul's pride existed first which allowed the entrance of jealousy. It erupted when the women of the land sang of David's accomplishments as greater than King Saul's. At that moment, the infection spread in Saul's heart against David.

**When we try to deal with rage, we are actually only dealing with a symptom.**

Pride always brings a host of minions with it. Let's look at the progression: pride, to jealousy, to offense, which invites deception which stirs anger that bursts into rage. Saul could have halted the progression at any time. Instead he chose to let it incubate in his mind and heart until it consumed him and drove him.

As we go about our day, we will no doubt encounter this rage at some time or another. It can rise up at the most unexpected moment and from the most unexpected source. But when that rage tries to engage us, don't. Remember, it is a call to prayer for those involved as well as for our own hearts to keep them out of offense.

**Remember, anger is simply an indicator.** But if left unchecked it will always turn to rage which blinds eyes to truth and works to bring about destruction.

But rage isn't the last step of the progression. Sadly, there is more and it gets worse.

# SCRIPTURES

*Everyone should be quick to listen, slow to speak and slow to become angry, because human anger does not produce the righteousness that God desires.* (James 1:19-20)

*In your anger do not sin: Do not let the sun go down while you are still angry, and do not give the devil a foothold. Anyone who has been stealing must steal no longer, but must work, doing something useful with their own hands, that they may have something to share with those in need.*

*Do not let any unwholesome talk come out of your mouths, but only what is helpful for building others up according to their needs, that it may benefit those who listen. And do not grieve the Holy Spirit of God, with whom you were sealed for the day of redemption. Get rid of all bitterness, rage and anger, brawling and slander, along with every form of malice.* (Ephesians 4:26-31)

*Fools give full vent to their rage, but the wise bring calm in the end.* (Proverbs 29:11)

*Be not quick in your spirit to become angry, for anger lodges in the heart of fools.* (Ecclesiastes 7:9 ESV)

*A gentle answer turns away wrath, but a harsh word stirs up anger.* (Proverbs 15:1)

*A hot-tempered person stirs up conflict, but the one who is patient calms a quarrel.* (Proverbs 15:18)

*But now you also, put them all aside: anger, wrath, malice, slander, and abusive speech from your mouth. Do not lie to one another, since you laid aside the old self with its evil practices, and have put on the new self who is being renewed to a true knowledge according to the image of the One who created him.* (Colossians 3:8-10 NASB)

*Cease from anger and forsake wrath; do not fret; it leads only to evildoing. For evildoers will be cut off, but those who wait for the Lord, they will inherit the land.* (Psalm 37:8-9 NASB)

*People with understanding control their anger; a hot temper shows great foolishness.* (Proverbs 14:29 NLT)

## Chapter 6

# IM GOING TO KILL YOU

The more success David achieved as a warrior for King Saul in biblical times, the greater the jealousy and more obsessed the king became with the desire to kill him. Think about that. His very best warrior. His son-in-law. A man who supported King Saul in every detail, and yet the king was so consumed with the intent to kill David that he often left his kingdom and its people exposed as he took his army out to hunt David. It proved to be a wild goose chase as God protected David so that Saul couldn't touch him.

We can see this demonic progression in America today. Pride and disagreement against a political belief, religious belief, moral belief, etc. have erupted; and the result has been fires of offense and rage that have broken out all across our land both physically and spiritually.

And I'm not just talking about one political group over another. It is everywhere. We've all seen the hate-filled rhetoric on social media sites in which nonbelievers state their rebuke of a person, candidate or Christian only to be told they are "garbage" or "I hope you go to Hell" comments by so-called Christians. What is that? Because it is not from God, but reveals another spirit.

These raging emotions, as they progress, eventually build until they become a murderous spirit. Mind you, it is not always the physical action of murder; it can be a murderous intent to destroy a business, a social media platform, a reputation, a friendship, etc.—much as the Left has been *consumed* in their effort to destroy and remove President Trump. Just as King Saul left his subjects exposed as he hunted David, so those consumed with removing Trump have often abandoned their work and duty to serve Americans as they spend their time and effort to overthrow the president. To them it seems reasonable, but their actions are driven by the virus.

**Raging emotions, as they progress, eventually build until they become a murderous spirit.**

Once the virus reaches this stage, those infected are convinced that they are acting with honor and doing what is right. Why? Because remember, the spirit of deception is present which blinds all those in its grasp.

Look at the Pharisees.

The Pharisees in Jesus' day were so completely convinced of their religious right, propriety and education (pride) that as they plotted to kill Jesus, they were convinced in their own minds that they were doing a good thing. It was the exact same spirit that controlled Saul who later became Paul.

Saul was a highly educated religious leader, zealous for the things of God. But pride, because of his education and upbringing, had infected him with this spiritual virus. He was convinced that his pursuit of Jesus' disciples and his efforts to put them to death was in fact performing God's work. It took a divine intervention in which he was struck blind for three days for God to get his attention. Once the physical blindness was removed, so was the spiritual blindness. Then with the same passion in which he had formerly persecuted Christians, he now preached the Gospel of Jesus Christ. Although he was free of the virus personally, he recognized its presence everywhere he went. It became his consuming passion to help people get free.

Almost every single place Paul went, he encountered groups and mobs consumed by the virus not just opposing him, but intent on killing him. They followed him from one city to the next in their effort to discredit and harm him. Why? Because this is a spiritual virus and those infected are controlled and consumed by it to steal, kill and destroy, only they see it as an act of "social justice."

When in Jerusalem, Saul, now known as Paul, pleaded with the people to listen to him and to recognize the virus. He thought it would be evident to them. They all knew who he had once been and the zeal which had consumed him to persecute those with whom he now worked. His transformation should have been clear. But it wasn't—because they were infected and blinded as he once was.

**He encountered groups and mobs
consumed by the virus
not just opposing him,
but intent on killing him.**

He reminded them, *"I am a Jew, born in Tarsus of Cilicia, but brought up in this city. I studied under Gamaliel and was thoroughly trained in the law of our ancestors. I was just as zealous for God as any of you are today. I persecuted the followers of this Way to their death, arresting both men and women and throwing them into prison, as the high priest and all the Council can themselves testify. I even obtained letters from them to their associates in Damascus, and went there to bring these people as prisoners to Jerusalem to be punished."*[32]

He went on to share his experience, blinded by a light from Heaven and how he heard a voice tell him to go to Damascus. It was there that he was delivered from the control of the virus.

*"A man named Ananias came to see me. He was a devout observer of the law and highly respected by all the Jews living there. He stood beside me and said, 'Brother Saul, receive your sight!' And at that very moment I was able to see him.*

*"Then he said: 'The God of our ancestors has chosen you to know his will and to see the Righteous One and to hear words from his mouth. You will be his witness to all people of what you have seen and heard. And now what are you waiting for? Get up, be baptized and wash your sins away, calling on his name.'*

*"When I returned to Jerusalem and was praying at the temple, I fell into a trance and saw the Lord speaking to me. 'Quick!' he said. 'Leave Jerusalem*

*immediately, because the people here will not accept your testimony about me.'*

*"'Lord,' I replied, 'these people know that I went from one synagogue to another to imprison and beat those who believe in you. And when the blood of your martyr Stephen was shed, I stood there giving my approval and guarding the clothes of those who were killing him.'"*[33]

He thought that as he reminded people of his background, they would surely see the truth. But instead, his words enraged them, because the progression of the virus had already gone from pride, jealousy, offense, deception, anger, rage to murderous intent. They would stop at nothing to achieve their purpose. But what had Paul done deserving of death? Absolutely nothing. He simply held a different worldview.

Is this any different than the political arena in America today and those who relentlessly work to denounce or destroy President Trump? Blindly consumed, this is their goal just as the Pharisees were consumed with their goal to get rid of Jesus in their day. (Note: I'm not comparing President Trump to Jesus. I'm comparing the murderous intent that was present in leaders of that day compared to leaders of today.)

Jesus was gaining in popularity. They were losing popularity. Their jealousy and offense led to deception and they were enraged. The progression of the virus then went to the next stage of murderous intent.

**He thought that as he reminded people of his background, they would surely see the truth.**

Rage, like anger, is simply an indicator that points to the next stage of murderous intent which has been unleashed in increasing measures. Let's look at this through the recent Black Lives Matter movement.

There is no question or debate that black lives matter. But there also should be no question or debate that *all* lives matter. Remember the young woman I mentioned earlier who said it hurt her when people said "all lives matter?" What she heard with those words is that black lives *don't* matter. What causes that kind of disconnect? Because we've all had it. Unhealed hurts, wounds and offense cause us to hear and see through that filter so that what is said isn't what is heard.

I remember talking with a friend who I didn't realize at the time had offense against me. I spoke a word complimenting their skill in an area. Unfortunately, what they heard lodged in their mind as an insult, as the words went through a filter of offense. When I saw them a few weeks later, they had meditated on the perceived insult and the offense was now at huge proportions. When I asked them why they were so angry with me, they mentioned the comment. "That's not what I said at all," I responded.

"Yes, you did. I was there," they insisted.

Recognizing that I was dealing with an offense, I replied, "I'm so sorry. What I *meant* to say was. . . ." Then I delivered the compliment regarding their skill which I admired. However, the apology and compliment fell on deaf ears.

"That's not what you mean at all," he retorted angrily. "What you said originally is what you meant. Don't try to change it now!"

Whew! What do you do with that? No amount of apology, no matter how sincere, could undo the offense-laden opinion of my friend. It is the same spirit that came from the dear young woman who was wounded when she heard people say "not only do black lives matter, all lives matter." When hurt and offense are present, it twists what we hear and see.

I will continue to press the envelope by using the Black Lives Matter Movement as I discuss the virus, as the movement at its foundation has nothing to do with addressing the issue of racism, but is steeped in Marxism and destruction of biblical morality and the American family. It's a movement that has manipulated the wounds of the black community and the injustices they have experienced past or present and worked to stoke a fire of pride and offense which has led to deception that all police are evil and we must remove them. The "fruit" of this deception is evident in the riots and attacks—anger, rage and murderous intent. Do you see the progression of the virus?

**When hurt and offense are present, it twists what we hear and see.**

A month before the George Floyd issue, I wrote an article which described some incredible opportunities for the black community in Tulsa. It involved the restoration of Black Wall Street via opportunity zones. It was an amazing opportunity to restore what had been stolen. Perhaps you aren't aware that there was a Black Wall Street. There was and it was the most prosperous African-American community in America in 1921.

However, within hours it was gone, ravaged by a white mob.

According to History.com, Black Wall Street was comprised of luxury shops, restaurants, grocery stores, hotels, jewelry and clothing stores, movie theaters, barbershops/salons, a library, pool halls, night clubs, and offices for doctors, lawyers and dentists. Less affluent African-Americans lived there as well, working as janitors, dishwashers and domestics. It had its own school system, post office, bank and hospital. Money earned outside of Greenwood was spent within the district where every dollar changed hands approximately *nineteen times* before it left the community. [34]

But all of that disappeared in a mere eighteen hours when virtually every building in a forty-two-square-block area of the community was destroyed.

According to news documents, a black teenage shoe shiner was accused of sexually assaulting a white female elevator operator. The story spread quickly and almost immediately escalated to violence. The shoe shiner was jailed. As word circulated of plans to lynch him, a crowd showed up at the courthouse. A confrontation between the white community and the black community quickly spread to the Greenwood District of north Tulsa. Homes, schools, churches and businesses were burned to the ground. Reports estimated 300 black Tulsans were massacred and approximately 8,000 left homeless and penniless."[35]

Thousands of African-Americans spent the winter of 1921-1922 living in tents. In the end, no charges were filed against the African-American teen. Although reports vary, it is believed he tripped and bumped into the female elevator operator, causing her to scream, leading to the sexual assault allegation. As word spread, the story grew. The senseless massacre that destroyed Black Wall Street was in part the result of an article published in the city newspaper carried by word of mouth. Fear turned to hysteria sparking a rampage for "justice." That is the power of the media as the story spread fear and outrage. Unfortunately, it was fake news.

The effect was the spiritual infection took hold and began spreading faster than the news story. Pride, offense, deception, anger and rage to murderous intent. An entire community was decimated, businesses destroyed and hundreds murdered. Tragically, Black Wall Street has never been restored.

This tragedy shows how quickly we can be stirred into a murderous rage because we believe something to be true and take offense without waiting for facts. In pride we believe we are right and must execute justice.

Fast forward to George Floyd.

Since Floyd's death in Minneapolis, rioters have flooded the streets burning and looting buildings—some owned by black business owners. Why? It hasn't brought justice. But it has resulted in more needless deaths. That is the nature of this virus. It always brings destruction.

**The effect was the spiritual infection took hold and began spreading faster than the news story.**

While we know the Tulsa Race Massacre was due to racism, what do we know about Floyd's murder? That question may anger some, but if we call it racism simply because one of the four police officers was white and the victim black—that statement in and of itself is racist. We have made an assumption and judgment based on skin color rather than the facts which actually took place. When we do that, we have watered the spirit of offense which will always then move into anger and rage for "justice." Wasn't that exactly the same spirit behind the Tulsa Race Massacre? The belief that an injustice had occurred and had to be rectified? That is the danger when this virus controls our actions. It will always result in error and death.

## RECONCILIATION

While rage brings division, peace brings reconciliation. That is our call. This is a time for fervent intercession as rage and this murderous spirit which has been released continues to stir division. We will see it increase in days ahead. But it is time to arise, to build bridges to empower and unite in prayer and action. We are to be a people who *"will rebuild the ancient ruins and will raise up the age-old foundations; you will be called Repairer of Broken Walls, Restorer of Streets with Dwellings."*[36]

Like Nehemiah in biblical days, we are to stand up and declare that the walls of America which have been broken down need to be restored. It is only as we reunite as Christians and Americans that we can rebuild them. It will take each one of us doing something to see that happen. But we each have the power to do something. We are called to unite as a Body for walls of protection and reconciliation as brother links arm with brother. That is the victory coming in the days ahead for those who will heed this word.

While it is impossible to talk logic to someone who is enraged because a spirit of deception is present, kindness and goodness can overcome it and turn the tide. It's the goodness of God that draws men to repentance.

**It is time to arise, to build bridges to empower and unite in prayer and action.**

It is time to rise up and speak out to declare reconciliation in our land. It is time to unite as Nehemiah did to empower those around him who had grown weary of the battle to take up their sword and stand together to rebuild the wall. (To learn more about the "Nehemiah Strategy" go to http://bit.ly/nehemiahstrategy.)

The battle we see building ensues because this is a battle of good versus evil. Even now, reconciliation is in the air where God is turning the hearts of the fathers back to the children and the children to the fathers. It is an hour when the millennial generation will embrace the senior generation and the seniors will embrace the millennials. We will look at the differences in which God has created us and rejoice in the different gifts, diversity and strength that we bring together when we are whole. We are a people called to stand as the Church, united, to bring God glory, not divided by skin color, gender, culture or political ideology.

It is now that we must stand and declare the spirit of reconciliation to come forth for the winds have started to blow. It is coming, but so is the battle. We need to be ready, and we have our call as many are already in the final stages of this virus—which leads to death.

# SCRIPTURES

*Do not take revenge, my dear friends, but leave room for God's wrath, for it is written: "It is mine to avenge; I will repay," says the Lord.* (Romans 12:19)

*For this is the message which you have heard from the beginning, that we should love one another; not as Cain, who was of the evil one and slew his brother. And for what reason did he slay him? Because his deeds were evil, and his brother's were righteous.* (1 John 3:11-12 NASB)

*Everyone who hates his brother is a murderer; and you know that no murderer has eternal life abiding in him. We know love by this, that He laid down His life for us; and we ought to lay down our lives for the brethren.* (1 John 3:15-16 NASB)

*But the things that proceed out of the mouth come from the heart, and those defile the man. For out of the heart come evil thoughts, murders, adulteries, fornications, thefts, false witness, slanders. These are the things which defile the man; but to eat with unwashed hands does not defile the man.* (Matthew 15:18-19 NASB)

*There are six things which the Lord `hates, yes, seven which are an abomination to Him: haughty eyes, a lying tongue, and hands that shed innocent blood, a heart that* *devises wicked plans, feet that run rapidly to evil, a false witness who utters lies, and one who spreads strife among brothers.* (Proverbs 6:16-19 NASB)

*Let no debt remain outstanding, except the continuing debt to love one another, for whoever loves others has fulfilled the law. The commandments, "You shall not commit adultery," "You shall not murder," "You shall not steal," "You shall not covet," and whatever other command there may be, are summed up in this one command: "Love your neighbor as yourself." Love does no harm to a neighbor. Therefore love is the fulfillment of the law.* (Romans 13:8-10)

## Chapter 7

# THE FINAL STAGE

America is already in the final stages of this deadly progression. Recent examples are numerous:

- A woman was refused a marriage license when she applied for one to marry her computer.

- Biological males are allowed to compete as females in sports events simply because they "identify" as a sex that biology says they are not.

- Parents have boasted of taking their children to drag queen library reading events where afterwards they allow their young children to lay on top of the transgender reader. They believe this is healthy interaction.

- A man fatally shot a shopper who made him stand in line at Family Dollar.

- A Kansas teen was taken into custody after covering himself in Ranch dressing and then went on a rampage damaging property and crashing a car.

- Fifty-seven million children have been aborted in the U.S. since Roe v. Wade. Now some states have legalized infanticide, killing babies at full term or who have already been born, and this has been touted as "progress."

This is not progress; it is insanity.

How many times a day have you said to yourself or to someone regarding a news event or a conversation you heard, "That's insane!" This spiritual virus has progressed to the very last stage in pandemic proportion so that insanity has taken over the minds, hearts and actions of a multitude. Let's look at the full length of the progression, first from a historical perspective.

The years 486 to 465 B.C. marked the reign and Persian Empire of King Ahasuerus (Xerxes I) and his queen, Esther. During his reign the king promoted one of his advisors, Haman, to a position above all others in the land. The people were instructed to pay homage to him whenever he went by and bow before him. But there was a Jew named Mordecai who refused. This infuriated Haman as it tweaked his pride. Enter the virus.

Almost immediately the virus progressed from pride and offense to deception and rage as, *"When Haman saw that Mordecai neither bowed down nor paid homage to him, Haman was filled with rage."*[37] Once infected, Haman was consumed with the desire to get rid of Mordecai.

**This spiritual virus has progressed to the very last stage in pandemic proportion.**

*"But he disdained to lay hands on Mordecai alone, for they had told him who the people of Mordecai were (Jews); therefore Haman sought to destroy all the Jews, the people of Mordecai, who were throughout the whole kingdom of Ahasuerus."*[38]

But as the virus progressed, it wasn't enough for Haman to kill Mordecai alone. In his virus-filled mind, it made perfect sense to him to kill *all* of Mordecai's people, the Jews. Filled with murderous intent, Haman then used his governmental position to trick the king into signing a law that would allow him to do just that. He lied to the king, positioning his request for an edict to kill the Jews, as something that was for the king's protection. (Where have we heard that lie: "This is for your protection"?) It was all a lie, but King Ahasuerus trusted Haman and checked into it no further. Haman now had full legal approval to murder an entire race of people as the virus continued to overtake him.

What Haman missed in his pride and deception was that he was coming against the people of God—the Jews. He also didn't realize the man he despised, Mordecai, was the queen's uncle, the man who had raised her after her parents' deaths. As the well-known proverb states, *"Pride goes before destruction, and a haughty spirit before a fall."[39]* Haman's fall was inevitable.

Once Esther learned of the edict that would allow the slaughter of the Jews, she called for a three-day fast and then went before the king to plead for her life and that of her people. She humbled herself before God as she fasted and prayed for deliverance from an evil law.

That very action is indicative of the day we are in. The virus has progressed to the point that many in governmental positions have used their power and influence to create laws to slaughter the innocent (abortion), but state that it is for the protection and safety of the mother. Or to shut down churches and houses of worship, saying it is "for our protection" from COVID. It is the same lying, murderous spirit in operation which seeks to destroy and deceives its host into such vile actions.

Many today are in great fear because this murderous spirit has infected multitudes and created mob scenarios to intimidate us. But make no mistake, this spirit has no true authority when we humble ourselves before the Lord as they did in the days of Esther. Esther and the Jews of that day could have succumbed to fear but they refused. Fear causes us to back away and make decisions through the filter that we must hold onto our lives. But the Bible never instructs us to desperately cling to our lives. It tells us to trust God and be willing to lay down our lives. Are we willing and able to truly trust Him that He is greater than the murderous spirit and insanity that have been unleashed against America?

**But make no mistake,
this spirit has no true authority
when we humble ourselves
before the Lord**

He is.

As we look back on the historical account of Esther, we see what went from a hopeless situation to a complete turnaround. After their three days of fasting and prayer, when they were done, spiritually something shifted. Esther took courage and went before the king, knowing it could mean death. Her bold actions, instead, produced justice and life.

*"So the king and Haman went in to feast with Queen Esther. And on the second day, as they were drinking wine after the feast, the king again said to Esther, 'What is your wish, Queen Esther? It shall be granted you. And what is your request? Even to the half of my kingdom, it shall be fulfilled.' Then Queen Esther answered, 'If I have found favor in your sight, O king, and if it please the king, let my life be granted me for my wish, and my people for my request. For we have been sold, I and my people, to be destroyed, to be killed, and to be annihilated. If we had been sold merely as slaves, men and women, I would have been silent, for our affliction is not to be compared with the loss to the king.' Then King Ahasuerus said to Queen Esther, 'Who is he, and where is he, who has dared to do this?' And Esther said, 'A foe and enemy! This wicked Haman!' Then Haman was terrified before the king and the queen.*

## Haman Is Hanged

*"And the king arose in his wrath from the wine-drinking and went into the palace garden, but Haman stayed to beg for his life from Queen Esther, for he saw that harm was determined against him by the king. And the king returned from the palace garden to the place where they were drinking wine, as Haman was falling on the couch where Esther was. And the king said, 'Will he even assault the queen in my presence, in my own house?' As the word left the mouth of the king, they covered Haman's face. Then Harbona, one of the eunuchs in attendance on the king, said, 'Moreover, the gallows that Haman has prepared for Mordecai, whose word saved the king, is standing at Haman's house, fifty cubits high.' And the king said, 'Hang him on that.' So they hanged Haman on the gallows that he had prepared for Mordecai. Then the wrath of the king abated."*[40]

Consider how in just a short amount of time, Haman's pride took him all the way through the progression of the virus to its end—insanity. Haman was completely consumed by the infection and his end is the end for all who will not receive the cure—death. Haman was hanged on the very gallows he built for Mordecai. King Saul was killed in battle and his kingdom given to the man he sought to destroy. What will happen in America to those who are infected and who have progressed to the last stage of the virus?

*"When the wicked thrive, so does sin, but the righteous will see their downfall."*[41]

That verse in *The Message* reads, *"When degenerates take charge, crime runs wild, but the righteous will eventually observe their collapse."*[42]

Can you see that America is firmly in the grasp of this virus which is far more dangerous than COVID-19? Crime is running wild and degenerates (those who have sunk to a condition below that which is normal) have tried to overthrow the government in their attempted coup. The first coup attempt (Lucifer's attempt to overthrow God) failed and so will this one as we humble ourselves before the Lord, renounce pride and repent. Only then can we stop the virus and see the plague of offense, deception, rage, murderous intent and insanity flee.

Although America is in the final phase of this progressive virus, it is not too late to see it reversed. For while the battle of pride, offense, rage, murderous spirit and insanity march forward at an unprecedented rate, **God is calling ministers of reconciliation to arise.**

**Although America is in the final phase of this progressive virus, it is not too late to see it reversed.**

That is our call—to be ministers of reconciliation to an infected world. To do that we must not remain silent, but instead remove a critical component that has put us in this dangerous place.

# SCRIPTURES

Because insanity is an infection that has taken over the mind, the scriptures below focus on the importance of our minds and protection against this stage.

*The mind governed by the flesh is death, but the mind governed by the Spirit is life and peace.* (Romans 8:6)

*In reference to your former manner of life, you lay aside the old self, which is being corrupted in accordance with the lusts of deceit, and that you be renewed in the spirit of **your mind**, and put on the new self, which in the likeness of God has been created in righteousness and holiness of the truth.* (Ephesians 4:22-24 NASB)

*Watch over **your heart** (and mind) with all diligence, for from it flow the springs of life. Put away from you a deceitful mouth and put devious speech far from you. Let your eyes look directly ahead and let your gaze be fixed straight in front of you. Watch the path of your feet and all your ways will be established.* (Proverbs 4:23-26 NASB)

*Do not conform to the pattern of this world, but be transformed by the renewing of **your mind.** Then you will be able to test and approve what God's will is—his good, pleasing and perfect will.* (Romans 12:2)

*Therefore if you have been raised up with Christ, keep seeking the things above, where Christ is, seated at the right hand of God. Set **your mind** on the things above, not on the things that are on earth.* (Colossians 3:1-2 NASB)

*Therefore put on the full armor of God, so that when the day of evil comes, you may be able to stand your ground, and after you have done everything, to stand. Stand firm then, with the belt of truth buckled around your waist, with the breastplate of righteousness in place, and with your feet fitted with the readiness that comes from the gospel of peace. In addition to all this, take up the shield of faith, with which you can extinguish all the flaming arrows of the evil one. And take **the helmet of salvation** and the sword of the Spirit, which is the word of God.* (Ephesians 6:13-17)

*Finally, brothers and sisters, whatever is true, whatever is noble, whatever is right, whatever is pure, whatever is lovely, whatever is admirable—if anything is excellent or praiseworthy—**think about** such things.* (Philippians 4:8)

## Chapter 8

# AMERICA BECAME A LAND OF IDOL WORSHIP

D o you have a golden calf sitting in your backyard that you worship? Yeah, me neither. The calf is what typically comes to mind with the word "idolatry," at least for me. In biblical days, after their leader Moses disappeared for over a month, the Israelites gave their gold to Aaron who then melted it down to create an idol. When Moses reappeared with the Ten Commandments, Aaron defended his actions telling Moses, "*So I told them, 'Whoever has any gold jewelry, take it off.' Then they gave me the gold, and I threw it into the fire, and out came this calf!*"[43]

While most of us don't have a golden calf in our backyard, many of us have a television in our living room which reflects one modern-day area that has created idols in our culture.

- Sports teams
- Hollywood stars
- Musicians and singers. Think about the show "American Idol." That is more accurate than most of us realize.
- Education
- Beauty
- Social status
- Financial standing

Perhaps you are smiling to yourself and think none of those apply to you, but idols can come in all sorts of shapes and sizes. Your home, your new car, your job, food or perhaps your children? Ouch! Let's touch on the latter.

A few years ago, well-known evangelical author, Jen Hatmaker, and her husband came out with a public announcement which stunned many in the Christian community. In a Facebook post, the best-selling author of "7" and "For the Love" announced that she had changed her beliefs. She proclaimed to people engaged in homosexuality and LGBTism (there was no "Q" added at that time), "There is nothing wrong with you."[44] Hatmaker received immediate praise and backlash for her announcement. She defended her statement with the explanation that she and her husband had studied the issue from a biblical perspective for the last year and had come to the conclusion that God had no problem with homosexuality and that it was not a sin. She went on to say she believed it was time the Church offered LGBT persons complete acceptance into the Christian community. The only problem with that statement is it offered unsanctified grace while it ignored the sin. Her new stand was not biblical, but worse, neither was she truthful in her announcement.

## Idols can come in all sorts of shapes and sizes.

What Jen and her husband didn't disclose at the time was the true root of the issue—their daughter had chosen a life of homosexuality.

So, what do we do when something or someone important to us goes against the biblical values that we have embraced? I agree with Hatmaker that we go back to the Word of God to study and verify what God has to say on the issue. But the problem develops when we refuse to accept what the Bible says and so adjust it to fit our ideology.

Many Christian parents today find themselves in that difficult quandary. Perhaps it's not homosexuality. Perhaps your child has chosen a heterosexual relationship of sex outside of marriage. Or adultery. Or perhaps an unsavory vocation that puts you in an awkward position. Do you just "accept them with arms wide open" and say nothing? Do you stand firm on the foundation of the Bible and risk potentially alienating your child? Or do you shift your theology to be inclusive of their choices?

**What do we do when something or someone important to us goes against the biblical values that we have embraced?**

With the latter, we elevate our children to a place of idolatry as we exalt the child over God's Word. This is called idolatry.

While I agree with Hatmaker's decision to research what the Bible says on the issue of homosexuality, her conclusion contradicted the Word of God. She also did not come clean in immediately announcing the reason for her shift—which was their daughter's choices.

We've all watched numerous Christian leaders shift their theology over this particular issue. But as they embrace their child, they have made the decision to no longer embrace what God says. Essentially, they have given permission to others involved in the sin to believe there are no consequences for their choices.

**We elevate our children
to a place of idolatry as we
exalt the child over God's Word.**

That is deceptive and dangerous, and the Bible is clear that we are held accountable for these actions. *"If anyone causes one of these little ones—those who believe in me—to stumble, it would be better for them to have a large millstone hung around their neck and to be drowned in the depths of the sea."*[45]

It isn't just in the area of homosexuality where idolatry of children can be seen. It can be seen when a business owner or church leader elevates their child to a high level position that they have neither earned nor have the experience to hold. I once heard a well-known minister announce how his grown prodigal son had returned to the Lord. "My son is brilliant," the man gushed from the pulpit as he announced how he almost immediately made him the vice president of the ministry leapfrogging him over faithful mature men and women who had served for decades and were spiritually and experientially much more prepared for the position. The minister's love for his child rose to a level of idolatry due to pride that created a response that others could see was insanity. You can see the progression of the virus in play.

The problem with Hatmaker's stand on her very public platform is she essentially gave permission to those who have struggled with a homosexual lifestyle and temptations to "go ahead. It's okay. It's not a sin." However, the Bible is clear that it is.

Jen believes we are to accept those who struggle with homosexuality with "arms wide open" calling it loving our neighbor. I agree up to a point. Yes, we are to accept people with arms wide open—but we must remain firm to recognize and speak out what is sin. Jesus did as He told them, "Go and sin no more." That applies to our personal lives as well as with others.

We cannot ignore that God calls it sin:

*The wrath of God is being revealed from heaven against all the godlessness and wickedness of people, who suppress the truth by their wickedness, since what may be known about God is plain to them, because God has made it plain to them. For since the creation of the world God's invisible qualities—his eternal power and divine nature—have been clearly seen, being understood from what has been made, so that people are without excuse. For although they knew God, they neither glorified him as God nor gave thanks to him, but their thinking became futile and their foolish hearts were darkened. Although they claimed to be wise, they became fools and exchanged the glory of the immortal God for images made to look like a mortal human being and birds and animals and reptiles.*

*Therefore God gave them over in the sinful desires of their hearts to sexual impurity for the degrading of their bodies with one another. They exchanged the truth about God for a lie, and worshiped and served created things rather than the Creator—who is forever praised. Amen.*

*Because of this, God gave them over to shameful lusts. Even their women exchanged natural sexual relations for unnatural ones. In the same way the men also abandoned natural relations with women and were inflamed with lust for one another. Men committed shameful acts with other men, and received in themselves the due penalty for their error.*

*Furthermore, just as they did not think it worth-while to retain the knowledge of God, so God gave them over to a depraved mind, so that they do what ought not to be done. They have become filled with every kind of wickedness, evil, greed and deprav-ity. They are full of envy, murder, strife, deceit and malice. They are gossips, slanderers, God-haters, insolent, arrogant and boastful; they invent ways of doing evil; they disobey their parents; they have no understanding, no fidelity, no love, no mercy.*

*Although they know God's righteous decree that those who do such things deserve death, they not only continue to do these very things but also approve of those who practice them.*[46]

So how does this apply to the spiritual virus? It is very much part of the progression because idolatry is when we have elevated something in our lives to a position above God, and we choose to make that the place from which we make decisions and what holds authority over us. Take a moment now to consider any area of your life which may have moved into a role of idol worship. Your job? Your bank account? Food? Your children? Your position in society? Your skin color? Your gender? Your free time? Your addiction? A sport's team?

What possesses your attention is what possesses you.

And when there is an area which has become dominant over God, we have inadvertently activated the root of the virus—pride. Before we move forward it is important to take an important step to allow God to remove any root of pride that may be present, whether we see it or not.

*Lord, reveal to me any area of my life that is out of order which I have elevated to a position over You. Forgive me and open my eyes. I give it to You now. I lay it down and turn it over to You. Take it, Lord, because my desire is that nothing takes the number one spot in my life but You.*

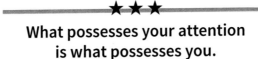

**What possesses your attention is what possesses you.**

Note: If there is an area of your life in which you are not willing to pray that prayer and turn it over to the Lord, it is the indicator that the area *is* an issue and has become an idol. Now let's look at the cure.

## Chapter 9

# THE CURE

I s there a vaccine for this spiritual virus? There is. It is found in the words, *"You shall know the truth, and the truth shall make you free."* [47] But how can we get to that place of truth if our mind is wrapped in deception from the virus?

To be cured, we must remove the infection at the root. Otherwise, we may temporarily put some symptoms at bay, like the couple we worked with in China, who repented of their anger and accusations at my husband and me, and yet within three days they were right back to the same rage. Why? Because the symptoms will return if the virus is not irradicated at the root.

This requires wisdom. In the verse below we learn how to be inoculated with this kind of wisdom, but it also reveals the presence of the virus.

## To be cured, we must remove the infection at the root.

*But if you have bitter jealousy and selfish ambition in your hearts, do not boast and be false to the truth. This is not the wisdom that comes down from above, but is earthly, unspiritual, demonic. For where jealousy and selfish ambition exist, there will be disorder and every vile practice. But the wisdom from above is first pure, then peaceable, gentle, open to reason, full of mercy and good fruits, impartial and sincere.*[48]

While there are a multitude of examples of the virus, which begins with pride, evident in historical accounts in the Bible, there are not nearly as many examples of those who broke free from the virus. Why? Because it requires that we lay down our pride and determination that we are right in order to break free.

King Nebuchadnezzar was one who did break free, but only by the grace of God. If you remember, he first received a warning that he was infected from his most trusted advisor, Daniel, known as Belteshazzar.

Nebuchadnezzar had a dream which none of his magicians or wise men could interpret. So he called for Daniel and said, *"Belteshazzar, chief of the magicians, I know that the spirit of the holy gods is in you, and no mystery is too difficult for you. Here is my dream; interpret it for me. These are the visions I saw while lying in bed: I looked, and there before me stood a tree in the middle of the land. Its height was enormous. The tree grew large and strong and its top touched the sky; it was visible to the ends of the earth. Its leaves were beautiful, its fruit abundant, and on it was food for all. Under it the wild animals found shelter, and the birds lived in its branches; from it every creature was fed.*

*"In the visions I saw while lying in bed, I looked, and there before me was a holy one, a messenger, coming down from heaven. He called in a loud voice: 'Cut down the tree and trim off its branches; strip off its leaves and scatter its fruit. Let the animals flee from under it and the birds from its branches. But let the stump and its roots, bound with iron and bronze, remain in the ground, in the grass of the field.*

*"'Let him be drenched with the dew of heaven, and let him live with the animals among the plants of the earth. Let his mind be changed from that of a man and let him be given the mind of an animal, till seven times pass by for him.*

*"'The decision is announced by messengers, the holy ones declare the verdict, so that the living may know that the Most High is sovereign over all kingdoms on earth and gives them to anyone he wishes and sets over them the lowliest of people.'*

*"This is the dream that I, King Nebuchadnezzar, had. Now, Belteshazzar, tell me what it means, for none of the wise men in my kingdom can interpret it for me. But you can, because the spirit of the holy gods is in you."*[49]

Remember, it is out of relationship that we truly have authority to speak into such a sensitive issue. The king came to Daniel and *asked* him for his insight. Once Daniel recognized the dream was a dire warning about the king, he was terrified. Because even though Daniel had every reason to hate the king, as he had him taken as a young man out of his own land and forced him to change his name and his culture to serve the king, Daniel had been obedient to faithfully pray for him. It's hard to pray for someone and hate them. That is unless we are praying *at* them rather than *for* them. Remember, the instruction to pray for those in authority over us doesn't mean we have to agree with them or their agenda. It just means we are to pray *for* them.

I learned this in a fresh way when I was invited to be on a small prayer team for an elected official with whom I did not agree with most of his political ideology. However, as I prayed for the official, and with him on several occasions with the team, something changed. We prayed for God to bless him, speak to him, give him wisdom and insight to lead wisely, etc. As I prayed, God gave me a deep love and compassion for him, even though I often disagreed with him! Instead of praying *at* him, where I prayed what I wanted to happen, I learned to pray *for* him, that God would guide his steps, give him wisdom and help him to lead for the benefit of the citizens. It was in that prayer role that I finally understood how Daniel could serve the ungodly King Nebuchadnezzar and say the following,

**It is out of relationship that
we truly have authority to speak
into such a sensitive issue.**

*"My lord, if only the dream applied to your enemies and its meaning to your adversaries!"*[50] When we truly humble ourselves and pray *for* our leaders, we will see them as God sees them rather than from any place of disagreement or judgment which seems paramount in our eyes.

Daniel led by example, and in the end, God used him to serve in four administrations because of his obedience.

**When we truly humble ourselves
and pray for our leaders,
we will see them as God sees them.**

As Daniel stood before the king, he interpreted the dream. *"The tree you saw, which grew large and strong, with its top touching the sky, visible to the whole earth, with beautiful leaves and abundant fruit, providing food for all, giving shelter to the wild animals, and having nesting places in its branches for the birds—Your Majesty, you are that tree! You have become great and strong; your greatness has grown until it reaches the sky, and your dominion extends to distant parts of the earth.*

*"Your Majesty saw a holy one, a messenger, coming down from heaven and saying, 'Cut down the tree and destroy it, but leave the stump, bound with iron and bronze, in the grass of the field, while its roots remain in the ground. Let him be drenched with the dew of heaven; let him live with the wild animals, until seven times pass by for him.'*

*"This is the interpretation, Your Majesty, and this is the decree the Most High has issued against my lord the king: You will be driven away from people and will live with the wild animals; you will eat grass like the ox and be drenched with the dew of heaven. Seven times will pass by for you until you acknowledge that the Most High is sovereign over all kingdoms on earth and gives them to anyone he wishes. The command to leave the stump of the tree with its roots means that your kingdom will be restored to you when you acknowledge that Heaven rules. Therefore, Your Majesty, be pleased to accept my advice: Renounce your sins by doing what is right, and your wickedness by being kind to the oppressed. It may be that then your prosperity will continue."*

Daniel understood how to be free of the virus, because he had taken those steps years before when abducted from his homeland. Rather than remain in unforgiveness and offense, and rather than take pride in his position as the wisest advisor to the king, he remained humble before the Lord and others. He was virus-free. After interpreting the dream for the king, he advised him how to be free as well and how to avoid the penalty that was headed his way. Unfortunately, the king was unable to heed that wise advice.

## The Dream Is Fulfilled

*All this happened to King Nebuchadnezzar. Twelve months later, as the king was walking on the roof of the royal palace of Babylon, he said, "Is not this the great Babylon I have built as the royal residence, by my mighty power and for the glory of my majesty?"*

*Even as the words were on his lips, a voice came from heaven, "This is what is decreed for you, King Nebuchadnezzar: Your royal authority has been taken from you. You will be driven away from people and will live with the wild animals; you will eat grass like the ox. Seven times will pass by for you until you acknowledge that the Most High is sovereign over all kingdoms on earth and gives them to anyone he wishes."*

*Immediately what had been said about Nebuchadnezzar was fulfilled. He was driven away from people and ate grass like the ox. His body was drenched with the dew of heaven until his hair grew like the feathers of an eagle and his nails like the claws of a bird.*[51]

But God had mercy on Nebuchadnezzar and his sentence of judgment didn't end in death, but rather an opportunity to come back to his senses and escape out of the snare of pride.

*At the end of that time, I, Nebuchadnezzar, raised my eyes toward heaven, and my sanity was restored. Then I praised the Most High; I honored and glorified him who lives forever. His dominion is an eternal dominion; his kingdom endures from generation to generation. All the peoples of the earth are regarded as nothing. He does as he pleases with the powers of heaven and the peoples of the earth. No one can hold back his hand or say to him: "What have you done?"*

*At the same time that my sanity was restored, my honor and splendor were returned to me for the glory of my kingdom. My advisers and nobles sought me out, and I was restored to my throne and became even greater than before. Now I, Nebuchadnezzar, praise and exalt and glorify the King of heaven, because everything he does is right and all his ways are just. And those who walk in pride he is able to humble.*[52]

Just as God gave Nebuchadnezzar a warning before judgment took place, so God has been giving America—and all Americans—warning to repent of our pride to be free of this virus. However, we must recognize that there is never certainty that mercy will continue to be extended as Nebuchadnezzar experienced. There eventually comes a season in which people who do not repent do not return from the insanity of this virus. In those cases, the end result will be death as the virus runs its full course.

The key is once free of the infection to avoid reinfection.

Let's review the progression of the virus again: pride > jealousy > offense > deception > anger > rage > murderous intent > insanity > death.

**God has been giving America— and all Americans—warning to repent of our pride to be free of this virus.**

As you review the progression, are you able to see any of these issues present in your life? The problem is, because of deception, we usually don't.

## REMOVING THE ROOT

The key to removing the root and infection requires removing deception. "But I'm not deceived!" you insist. That is the very nature of deception: That we don't recognize when we are in it, and it doesn't feel real when people warn us that it is present in our lives.

Author and teacher, Kris Vallotton didn't feel he had deception operating in his life either until a friend took him aside.

"One day Danny (a personal friend and pastor) came into my office and said, 'I would like to talk to you for a couple of minutes. I actually have a counseling appointment in ten minutes, so I'm only going to have ten minutes to tell you. I don't want this to go on any longer. So, I'm just going to tell you and you work it out,'" Kris began.

The two sat down together and Danny continued, "For the sake of time, here's the struggle. You've got arrogance and pride on your life."

"That doesn't feel true," Kris responded. "I'm going to need some examples."

His friend gave him four examples from the last two months where he had seen arrogance and pride in Kris in meetings in which the two had attended. Vallotton bristled as he remembered each of the four meetings. In each of the instances, he felt he had reasons for his responses. He replied, "I don't agree with you."

His friend Danny stood to leave as he responded, "I don't have time to argue. That's my word to you."

While that may sound like a harsh statement, it's important to recognize it came from a sincere friend who loved Kris and from a strong relationship they had built over the years. It is only from relationship that we can speak such a word to someone.

Kris remembered how he went to bed that night feeling pretty discouraged as he considered how Danny considered him arrogant and prideful.

"I'm pretty good at saying 'I'm really sorry' and cleaning up my mess," Kris recounted,

"but the truth is I didn't see it. I thought, 'He's wrong.'"

As he lay in bed reviewing the conversation, the Lord spoke to his heart, "If you don't trust someone more than you trust yourself, then you can't get out of deception." Kris laughed and responded, "Lord, *I* said that!"

"Yes, you did!" the Lord replied.

Kris then asked Him, "Was Danny right?"

The response wasn't a "yes" or "no." Instead, He repeated the same phrase to Kris three times. "If you don't trust someone more than you trust yourself, you can't get out of deception."

**"If you don't trust someone more than you trust yourself, then you can't get out of deception."**

Kris pondered the situation as he lay in bed that night and thought, "Danny's absolutely wrong. I don't mind being wrong, but I'm not wrong. Not in this instance," he thought to himself. In his mind he went back over the four meetings and conversations his friend had referenced as part of the issue and yet still Kris said there didn't appear to be anything in them or himself that felt arrogant or prideful. He just didn't see it.

As he lay there, he had this thought, "Right now I have to make a choice. If it's true that I'm deceived, then what Danny shared with me won't feel real, which is one of the symptoms I have. So, it *is* possible that I'm deceived because it doesn't feel real and I've had twenty-five years with this man. He loves me and he cares about me and has been very accurate in my life. He would not tell me this to hurt me. He's been one of my very best friends in life and has no motive to hurt me."

Kris continued to process the situation. Since he had not been arrogant or prideful directly to Danny, Kris realized his friend wasn't coming to him in anger or with a personal hurt. There was absolutely no conflict of interest. In that moment he had to acknowledge that all the symptoms were present to indicate that he actually had a problem.

"So, I prayed this simple prayer," Kris continued. "'I choose to believe that Danny's right even though it doesn't feel true.' As I continued to lay there, I had no feeling or emotion. No God moment. Nothing besides I made a choice of my will to choose to believe him (Danny) even though it didn't feel true on any level."

Immediately following that prayer, within half a second, he saw each of those circumstances again. But this time he could see the arrogance and pride that was present in each one. He broke down and wept as he thought, "Oh my God, I made such a fool of myself."

"The second before I prayed that prayer, I could not see it," Kris finished. "I did not pray that prayer because I was broken or because I thought he was right, but only because I knew the principle of coming out of deception was true. As soon as I acknowledged that and said to the Lord, 'I will do what Danny tells me to do,' (he humbled himself which removed the pride—the root and deception) instantly it was like someone took dark glasses off my eyes."

Now as he revisited those four times, he could see his heart in each instance as he finally agreed, "Arrogance and pride were growing in my heart and I never saw it."

Kris says he wept through most of the night. He repented and then humbled himself first to God, and then the next day he went to each of the people who had been present when he had made those arrogant statements. He repented to each of them and then asked for forgiveness.[53]

It will only take doing that a few times before we become more alert to watch out for the insidious spirit of pride which can so easily infiltrate our minds.

### Instantly it was like someone took dark glasses off my eyes.

So, what is the vaccine, the cure for the virus? It is when we humble ourselves and repent. That is what removes the root—pride. This is why we are commanded, *"If my people, who are called by my name, will humble themselves and pray and seek my face and turn from their wicked ways, then I will hear from heaven, and I will forgive their sin and will heal their land."*[54]

That is the vaccine and urgent key to the hour in which we live in which deception has become so prevalent and has pitted son against father, daughter against mother, friend against friend, neighbor against neighbor. It is only as we acknowledge that we may have deception operating in our lives and then repent that the spiritual blinders, which blind us to truth, are peeled away so we can truly see the situation. Not from our perspective, but from God's.

Is it really that simple? It is.

Is it really that difficult? It is. Because in order to humble ourselves, we must first admit we might be in error and lay down anything that has exalted itself in our lives over God. It requires that we give all to Him. And this is where we come to the moment of truth regarding the virus.

Are you willing to take that step? To ask the Lord, "Is there any area of deception operating in my life? What am I missing?" And then sit for a moment and wait. And let Him begin to speak into your life with whatever He has to say.

**In order to humble ourselves, we must first admit we might be in error.**

How do we stop the global spread of rage, deception and insanity? If starts with us. It's not about pointing it out in someone else, but in dealing with ourselves first. And remember, if you do have a friend or family member who you recognize is caught in this spiritual virus, the first step is to pray *for* them, not at them.

**How do we stop the global spread of rage, deception and insanity? If starts with us.**

## WHAT CAN WE DO?

Our first step when we recognize that a family member or friend is infected is not to go and point it out! Remember the nature of deception. They won't be able to see it. It won't seem real to them, and they will most likely erupt in rage. The first step, once you have done the necessary work to ensure that you are virus-free, is to spend time fasting and praying for the individual. *Then* out of a spirit of love, it is time to discuss the presence of the virus. Remember, when we pray *for* someone rather than *at* someone God will fill our hearts with love and compassion for them. It is from that place, and out of relationship, that we can begin a discussion. Why is fasting and prayer an essential component? Because prayer is not enough.

> *Then the disciples came to Jesus privately and said, "Why could we not drive it out?" And He said to them, "Because of the littleness of your faith; for truly I say to you, if you have faith the size of a mustard seed, you will say to this mountain, 'Move from here to there,' and it will move; and nothing will be impossible to you.* **"But this kind does not go out except by prayer and fasting."**[55]

This is a spiritual virus, and we are dealing with a spirit force that must be removed.

I know the thought of going to someone to have this type of discussion is uncomfortable. Perhaps if you are reading this you are thinking to yourself, "I just want to pray and not say anything." I understand. But let's go back to the story of the man who tossed his garbage out of his car window as he placed his order. When we allow wrong actions and deception to continue, it does nothing to stop the virus or help the infected to be free of it. Instead they remain in torment. If we truly love, we will want to help others be free. But even more than that, we have a responsibility to speak to them.

*"Son of man, speak to your people and say to them: 'When I bring the sword against a land, and the people of the land choose one of their men and make him their watchman, and he sees the sword coming against the land and blows the trumpet to warn the people,*

*Then if anyone hears the trumpet but does not heed the warning and the sword comes and takes their life, their blood will be on their own head. Since they heard the sound of the trumpet but did not heed the warning, their blood will be on their own head. If they had heeded the warning, they would have saved themselves.*

*But if the watchman sees the sword coming and fails to blow the trumpet to warn the people and the sword comes and takes someone's life, that person's life will be taken because of their sin, but I will hold the watchman accountable for their blood.'*

*"Son of man, I have made you a watchman for the people of Israel, so hear the word I speak and give them warning from Me. When I say to the wicked, 'You wicked person, you will surely die,' and you do not speak out to dissuade them from their ways, that wicked person will die for their sin, and I will hold you accountable for their blood. But if you do warn the wicked person to turn from their ways and they*

*do not do so, they will die for their sin, though you yourself will be saved."*[56]

We *are* our brother's keeper. We are all watchmen. If we see there is someone infected by the virus and do nothing, we are held accountable for what happens to them. And we already know if the virus runs its course with no intervention, the end result is death. May we not stand back and remain silent when we have access and knowledge of the cure.

**If we see there is someone infected by the virus and do nothing, we are held accountable.**

Remember, it's the goodness of God that draws men to repentance. May we all operate from His goodness and kindness to see this pandemic obliterated from our land and across the world.

# HAVE YOU BEEN TESTED?

Are you infected? Do you or someone you know have the virus? If we don't know we are infected, we won't seek a cure. Here is a short test in which you can receive immediate results:

1. Do anger and rage dominate your thoughts as you listen to the news or conversations?

2. Do you often feel like you are the smartest person in the room?

3. Do you feel like those who disagree with you are below you and of lower intellect?

4. Do you feel it is necessary to ignore, unfriend or belittle those with whom you disagree?

5. Do you find yourself constantly and passionately critiquing or criticizing those of a different worldview, religion, sexual preference, economic position, gender, age group, culture, etc.?

6. Do you have a long trail of broken relationships, especially because of words or comments you have made?

7. Do you work to sabotage the efforts of those you dislike or disagree with rather than working to reconcile with them or engage in a discussion?

8. Do you feel corrupt people or leaders deserve what they get?

9. Do you feel that all things should be equal in every area of life and so whatever it takes to level the playing field is what you are compelled to do?

10. Do you believe that those who carry a different worldview have had fair warning to change, and whatever happens from this point on they deserve?

If you answered yes to one or more of these questions, it is quite possible you are infected in some area. It is important to follow through with the prayer to be virus-free on the following page.

# PRAYER TO BE VIRUS-FREE

*Lord, I ask that You would reveal any area of my life in which pride has entered and in which I am missing what is truly happening around me. It doesn't feel like that is the case. However, if it is, please reveal any area in which there is pride and deception which have kept me from seeing the truth. Help me to see the people and situations around me as You see them. Give me a humble heart to walk in Your way.*

*I command pride to leave and take its minions with it. I say no to pride, jealousy, offense, deception, anger, rage, insanity and death. As they leave, Lord, fill me with humility in place of pride, gratitude in place of jealousy, forgiveness in place of offense, truth in place of deception, peace in place of anger and rage, a sound mind in place of insanity and life in place of death.*

*I choose life. I choose You. And I choose to be free. In Jesus' name I pray.*

# PRAYER FOR SOMEONE ELSE TO BE VIRUS-FREE

*Lord, I pray for (insert name) and ask that You would peel back the veil that has brought deception and kept them from seeing the truth. Lord, You said that You would take a heart of stone and turn it to flesh. This is my prayer for them. Wherever their heart has become calloused, hard or full of pride, Lord, I ask that You would soften it so that they can see and hear the truth. Lord, I pray on their behalf for mercy. You said it is the goodness of God that draws men to repentance. May they encounter Your goodness and Your glory today so that they can walk free from the spirit of darkness that has deceived them.*

*I pray they will escape out of the snare of the devil that has deceived them to do his will. I pray that they will be renewed in the spirit of their mind, which after God is created in righteousness and true holiness. If they are holding unforgiveness or offense against any that they will forgive so that they will be set free.*

*Lord, I pray over (insert name) that pride must go and that as it leaves, it must take every one of its minions with it. Lord, I pray for (insert name) that any fear, anger/rage and deception that have controlled their actions would* dissipate so that they are filled with Your peace. For You have not given them a spirit of fear, but of power, love and a sound mind.

I declare over them: Pride, release them. Jealousy, be gone. Offense, leave. Deception, loose them from your hold. Anger and rage, go now. Insanity, let go of their heart and mind. And I declare death, you will have no victory here. Lord, I pray that they would have a divine encounter with You and with Your goodness. And I ask that You would fill them with humility, gratitude, forgiveness, truth, peace and a sound mind. And that they would embrace this new life as they receive Your life. In Jesus' name.

# A NOTE FROM THE AUTHOR

Thank you for reading *Infected: How to Stop the Global Spread of Rage, Deception and Insanity.* The Lord opened my eyes to this infection after I walked through a difficult wilderness season of life. It is in those times that we have two choices. We can either draw close to Him and receive healing and insight, or we can remain wounded and offended and remain in the wilderness. The Israelites died in the wilderness, unwilling to learn. May we not follow in their footsteps, but instead follow hard after God.

My prayer is that this book has been a blessing in some way. If so, or if you have additional questions, I would love to hear from you. You can reach me at:

Mail: P. O. Box 700515, Tulsa, OK 74170 U.S.A.
E-mail: karendeehardin@gmail.com
Or you can check out my websites and social media:
Business website: prioritypr.org
Personal website: karenhardin.com
Prophetic Insights: karenhardin.com/blog/
Facebook: www.facebook.com/karen.d.hardin.5
Facebook: www.facebook.com/PNPCHardin/
CloutHub: @karendeehardin

# ABOUT THE AUTHOR

 **Karen Hardin** is a writer, literary agent and cofounder of Destiny Builders, a nonprofit organization to the nations and to governmental leaders. She is a contributing writer for Intercessors for America and has been published in a number of publications including USA Today, Intercessors for America, Charisma, Elijah List, CBN.com, and more.

She has worked in publishing for over 25 years and is the president of PriorityPR Group & Literary Agency where she has worked with some of the most well-known names in the industry. Her passion is to help raise up others to recognize their identity and destiny.

She and her husband, Kevin, have worked extensively in Asia for the last thirty years. The last five years, Karen has been led to Washington, D.C. and the arena of government. She has spoken before the United Nations, been part of the National Prayer Breakfast and leads prayer tours in Washington, D.C.

For additional information, go to destinybuilders. world or to sign up for her weekly prophetic blog go to: karenhardin.com.

Karen has several online training webinars available to help take your writing to the next level and begin to build a writing resume.

- **Social Media Secrets: How to Increase Engagement and Get People to Listen**

This webinar focuses attention primarily toward Facebook and the various steps you can take to increase your response and build an audience.

- **6 Important and Money-Saving Tips You Need to Know BEFORE You Start Your Children's Book**

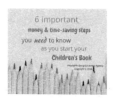

Writing a children's book seems simple, but in reality, there are more moving parts in this area than any other type of book. And what you don't know will definitely hurt you and cost an enormous amount of time and money.

- **Help! I Need a Publisher**

There are three types of publishers. This will tell you what you need to look for and what you need to avoid and help you determine which one is best for you.

- **From an Agent's Point of View**

This webinar will explain to you the quickest ways to get our attention and the quickest ways to turn us off as well as how to submit what an agent needs in order to review your manuscript and consider representing you.

- **Get Your Writing to the Next Level**

Six important techniques you need to know to take your writing from average to exceptional and how to do them.

- **Get Your Writing to the Next Level – Part 2**

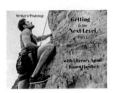

This webinar gets more into the nuts and bolts of publishing such as the 4 levels of edits, what makes a good cover, the pros and cons of CreateSpace, fonts, bar codes, etc.

- **The Easiest Way to Get Published and Build Your Platform at the Same Time!**

This is one of the most helpful and practical webinars for writers who want to build their writing resume and platform. This will teach you how to write short articles and how to get them published regularly along with the best strategy for results. Never been published? That can all change with this training.

For additional information on how to get published, or to download a proposal to submit your manuscript, go to: www.prioritypr.org

Karen has several free scriptural prayers available for download which include:

- He Will Provide: Scriptural Prayer Decrees for Provision

- Secure the Borders of Your Home: Scriptural Prayer Decrees for You and your Family

- Prayer of Confession and Repentance and a Cry for Revival

- Prayer of Breakthrough for America

- In Times of Famine – Scripture Prayer Decree for Provision - 2

To get your copy go to: https://destinybuilders. world/download-prayer/

## Washington, D.C. Prayer Tour

Photo credit: Our Time in History

Are you interested in joining us on a prayer team to Washington, D.C.? If so go to: https://destinybuilders. world/dc-prayer-tours/

# ENDNOTES

## Endorsements
[1] NKJV

## Chapter 1
[2] Kelley Paul, *Kelley Paul: Our Harrowing, Dystopian Night*, Washington Examiner, August 28, 2020. https://www. washingtonexaminer.com/opinion/op-eds/kelley-paul-the-most-harrowing-night-of-my-life Accessed August 31, 2020.
[3] Bryan Brammer, Group viciously attacks customer outside TX store: "Kicked me in the face and said, 'Black Lives Matter,'" Disrn News, June 17, 2020, https://disrn.com/news/group-viciously-attacks-customer-outside-tx-store-kicked-me-in-the-face-and-said-black-lives-matter, Accessed October, 9 2020.
[4] Joseph Guzman, Viral videos show protesters demanding DC restaurant patrons raise fists in solidarity,
The Hill, August 25, 2020 https://thehill.com/changing-america/respect/513646-viral-videos-show-protesters-demanding-dc-restaurant-patrons-raise. Accessed October 9, 2020.

## Chapter 2
[5] Acts 19:23-41
[6] Acts 19:25
[7] Isaiah 14:12-15 ESV.
[8] I Peter 5:5 NKJV.
[9] Ronald McDonald, "The Secretly Prideful Person," Saddleback Leather Company, https://saddlebackleather.com/signs-of-pride Accessed October 14, 2020.
[10] Definition of resist, http://webstersdictionary1828.com/Dictionary/resist. Accessed July 8, 2020.
[11] Proverbs 16:18 NKJV.

[12] Encyclopedia Britannica Editors, "Pharisee – Jewish History," Encyclopedia Britannica Online, https://www.britannica.com/topic/Pharisee. Accessed October 14, 2020.

[13] Psalm 86:14.

[14] 1 Samuel 18:7.

[15] Matthew 24:24 NASB.

[16] John 16:2 NASB.

[17] Psalm 139:23-24 KJV.


Chapter 3

[18] Steve Watson, Study Reveals that Easily Offended People are Less Productive, "Summit News," July 6, 2020, https://summit.news/2020/07/06/study-reveals-that-easily-offended-people-are-less-productive-bad-employees/ Accessed July 9, 2020.

[19] Proverbs 4:23 NKJV.

[20] Ephesians 6:12.

[21] Jonathan Martin and Alan Rappeport, "Donald Trump Says John McCain Is No War Hero, Setting Off Another Storm," The New York Times, July 18, 2015, https://www.nytimes.com/2015/07/19/us/politics/trump-belittles-mccains-war-record.html. Accessed October 17, 2020.

[22] Julian Borger, "John McCain Passes Dossier Alleging Secret Trump-Russia Contacts to FBI," The Guardian, January 11, 2017, https://www.theguardian.com/us-news/2017/jan/10/fbi-chief-given-dossier-by-john-mccain-alleging-secret-trump-russia-contacts. Accessed October 17, 2020.

[23] Eugene Scott, "McCain's Critiques of Trump have President's Supporters Angry and Firing Back, The Washington Post, May 7, 2018, https://www.washingtonpost.com/news/the-fix/wp/2018/05/07/mccains-critiques-of-trump-have-presidents-supporters-angry-and-firing-back/ Accessed October 17, 2020.

[24] Sinatra, Frank. "My Way." By Paul Anka. My Way, Reprise Records, 1969. LP.

[25] Ephesians 4:31-32

Chapter 4

[26] Luke 4:5-8

[27] Matthew 4:5-7 NASB.

[28] Margaret Sanger. The Pivot of Civilization (New York: Brentano's Publishers, 1922).

[29] Jason L. Riley, The Wall Street Journal, https://www.wsj.com/articles/lets-talk-about-the-black-abortion-rate-1531263697 Accessed October 17, 2020.


Chapter 5

[30] Mark Twain quote, Brainy Quote, https://www.brainyquote.com/quotes/mark_twain_120156. Accessed October 23, 2020.

[31] Ephesians 4:26.


Chapter 6

[32] Acts 22:3-5.

[33] Acts 22:12-20.

[34] Tulsa Race Massacre, History.com, March 8, 2018, https://www.history.com/topics/roaring-twenties/tulsa-race-massacre, Accessed October 20, 2020.

[35] Janice Ponds and Karen Hardin, "The Scapegoat: Finding the Truth Beyond Political Affiliations" Paladin Publishing, 2020.

[36] Isaiah 58:12.


Chapter 7

[37] Esther 3:5 NASB.

[38] Esther 3:6 NASB.

[39] Proverbs 16:18.

[40] Esther 7:1-10 ESV.

[41] Proverbs 29:16.

[42] Proverbs 29:16 MSG.


Chapter 8

[43] Exodus 32:24.

[44] Jen Hatmaker https://www.facebook.com/permalink.php?story_fbid=946752262090436&id=203920953040241, Accessed August 29, 2020.
[45] Matthew 18:6.
[46] Romans 1:18-32.

Chapter 9
[47] John 8:32 NKJV.
[48] James 3:14-17 ESV.
[49] Daniel 4:9-18.
[50] Daniel 4:19.
[51] Daniel 4:20-33.
[52] Daniel 4:34-37.
[53] Kris Vallotton, "How to Stay Out of Deception, August 16, 2009. https://www.youtube.com/watch?v=PimP9dVN1TU, Accessed October 24, 2020.
[54] 2 Chronicles 7:14.
[55] Matthew 17:19-21 NASB.
[56] Ezekiel 33:2-9.